STECK-VAUGHN

Mastering Math

Program Consultants

Robert Abbott
Assistant Director of Special Education
Waukegan Community Unit School District No. 60
Waukegan, Illinois

Marie Davis
Principal, McCoy Elementary School
Orange County Public Schools
Orlando, Florida

Monika Spindel
Teacher of Mathematics
Austin, Texas

Suzanne H. Stevens
Specialist in Learning Disabilities
Learning Enhancement Consultant
Winston-Salem, North Carolina

STECK-VAUGHN COMPANY
ELEMENTARY • SECONDARY • ADULT • LIBRARY

Table of Contents

◆ **Chapter 1: Numbers Through 10** — 1
  Problem Solving: Use a Picture — 16
◆ **Chapter 2: Addition Facts Through 10** — 23
  Problem Solving: Use a Picture — 38
◆ **Chapter 3: Subtraction Facts Through 10** — 45
  Problem Solving: Find a Pattern — 60
◆ **Cumulative Review: Chapters 1–3** — 67
◆ **Chapter 4: Place Value Through 99** — 75
  Problem Solving: Find a Pattern — 90
◆ **Chapter 5: Addition and Subtraction Facts Through 12** — 97
  Problem Solving: Use a Pictograph — 112
◆ **Chapter 6: Adding and Subtracting 2-Digit Numbers** — 119
  Problem Solving: Use a Bar Graph — 134
◆ **Cumulative Review: Chapters 4–6** — 141
◆ **Extra Practice:**
  Chapter 1 — 147
  Chapter 2 — 149
  Chapter 3 — 151
  Chapter 4 — 153
  Chapter 5 — 155
  Chapter 6 — 157

Acknowledgments

Executive Editor
Elizabeth Strauss

Project Editor
Donna Rodgers

Design Manager
John Harrison

Product Development
Colophon Publishing Services
Cary, North Carolina

Contributing Writers
Brantley Eastman, Diane Crowley, Mary Hill, Louise Marinilli, Harriet Stevens, Susan Murphy, Helen Coleman, Ann McSweeney

Product Design
The Quarasan Group, Inc.

ISBN 0-8114-3229-7
Copyright © 1994 Steck-Vaughn Company
All rights reserved. No part of the material protected by this copyright may be reproduced or utilized in any form or by any means, electronic or mechanical, including photocopying, recording, or by any information storage and retrieval system, without permission in writing from the copyright owner. Requests for permission to make copies of any part of the work should be mailed to: Copyright Permissions, Steck-Vaughn Company, P.O. Box 26015, Austin, TX 78755. Printed in the United States of America.
4 5 6 7 8 9 DBH 98 97

Illustration
Elizabeth Allen: pages T29, 6, 7, 12, 13, 15, 56, 57, 59, 67, 68, 78, 79, 83, 92, 95, 98, 99, 102, 103, 107, 108, 109, 111, 115, 123, 125, 127, 129, 131, 143, 155   Ben Anglin: pages 16, 24, 32, 33, 34, 35, 39, 61, 72, 91, 140, 144, 152, 156   Ruth Brunke: pages 8, 9, 37, 46, 47, 54, 55, 67, 76, 77, 81, 85, 86, 87, 92, 95, 100, 101, 106, 121, 133, 141, 153   Rhonda Childress: pages 55, 60, 64, 66, 69, 74, 85, 90, 112, 113, 116, 118, 131   David Griffin: pages 17, 20, 22, 35, 38, 42, 44, 134, 135, 148, 150, 158   Rich Lo: money   Kathryn Weldin: pages 2, 3, 4, 5, 10, 11, 18, 19, 25, 26, 27, 29, 30, 31, 48, 49, 50, 51, 52, 53, 67, 68, 104, 105, 115, 117, 147

Photography
© Myrleen Ferguson/PhotoEdit: page 45
© Tony Freeman/PhotoEdit: page 119
© Tom McCarthy/Unicorn Stock Photos: page 23
© Larry Migdale: pages 1, 75, 97

Cover Photography
Cooke Photographics

Name _____

CHAPTER 1

Numbers Through 10

The coach is helping the team get ready.
How many players have hats?
How many players still need hats?
How many bats do they have?

1

1

One and Two

How many?

| 1 one | 2 two |

Guided Practice

◆ Circle how many.

① 2	1 2
1 2	1 2
1 2	1 2

Practice

◆ Write 1 and 2.

1 1 1 1 . .

2 2 2 2 . .

◆ Write how many.

1

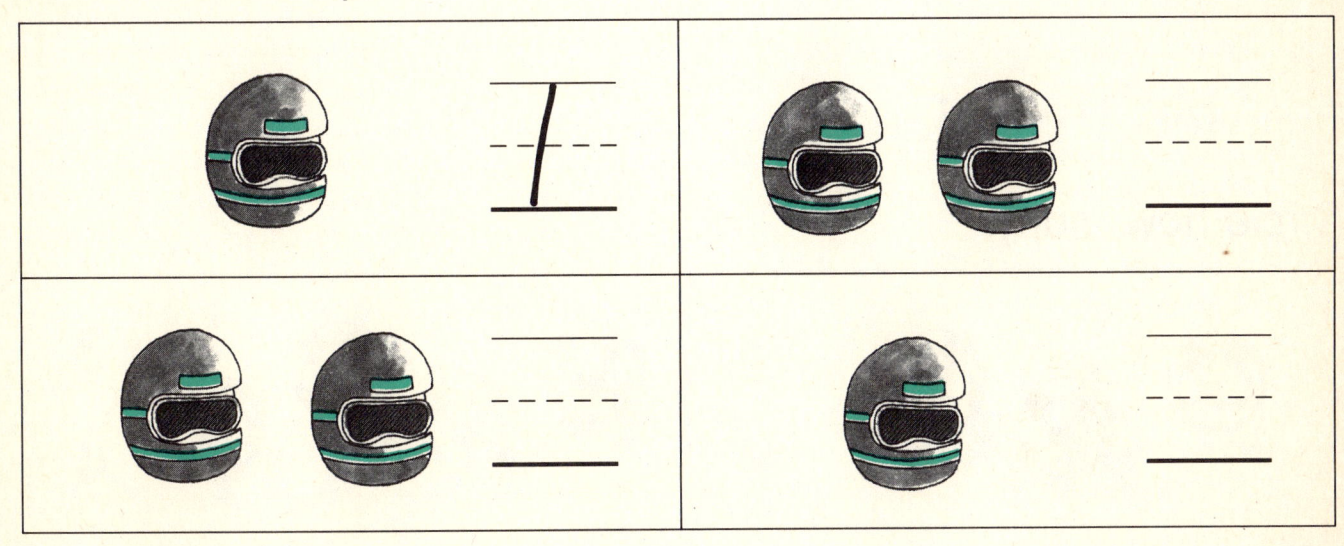

Using Math

◆ This is a 🖐 .

Write how many. ___

3

2

Three and Four

How many?

| 3 three 🏐🏐🏐 | 4 four 🏐🏐🏐🏐 |

Guided Practice

◆ Circle how many.

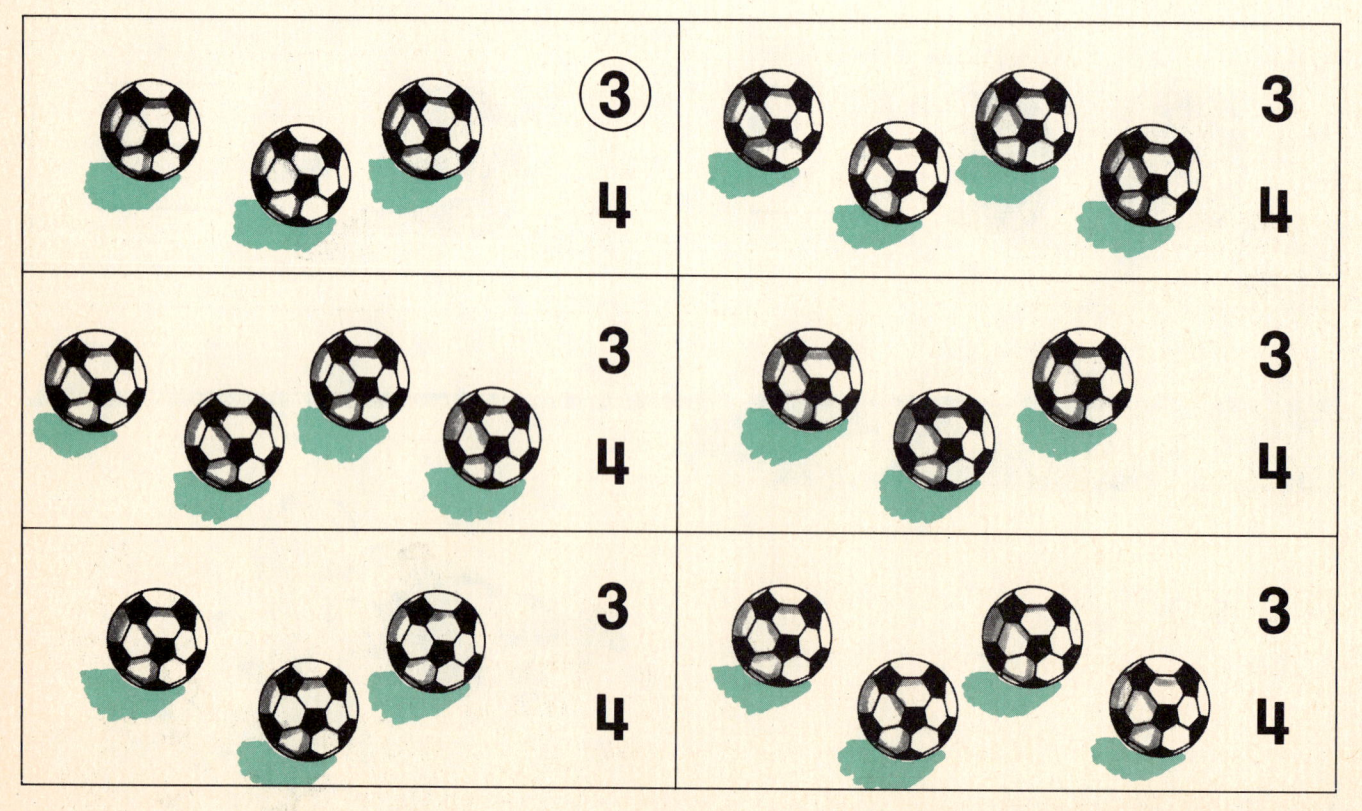

🏐🏐🏐	③ 4	🏐🏐🏐🏐	3 4
🏐🏐🏐🏐	3 4	🏐🏐🏐	3 4
🏐🏐🏐	3 4	🏐🏐🏐🏐	3 4

4

Practice

◆ Write 3 and 4.

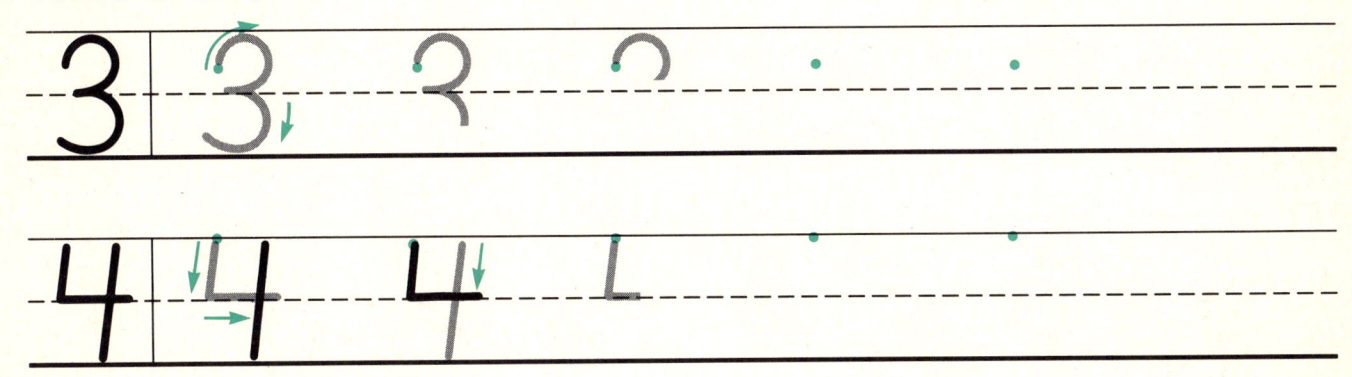

3 3 3 3 . .

4 4 4 4 L

◆ Write how many.

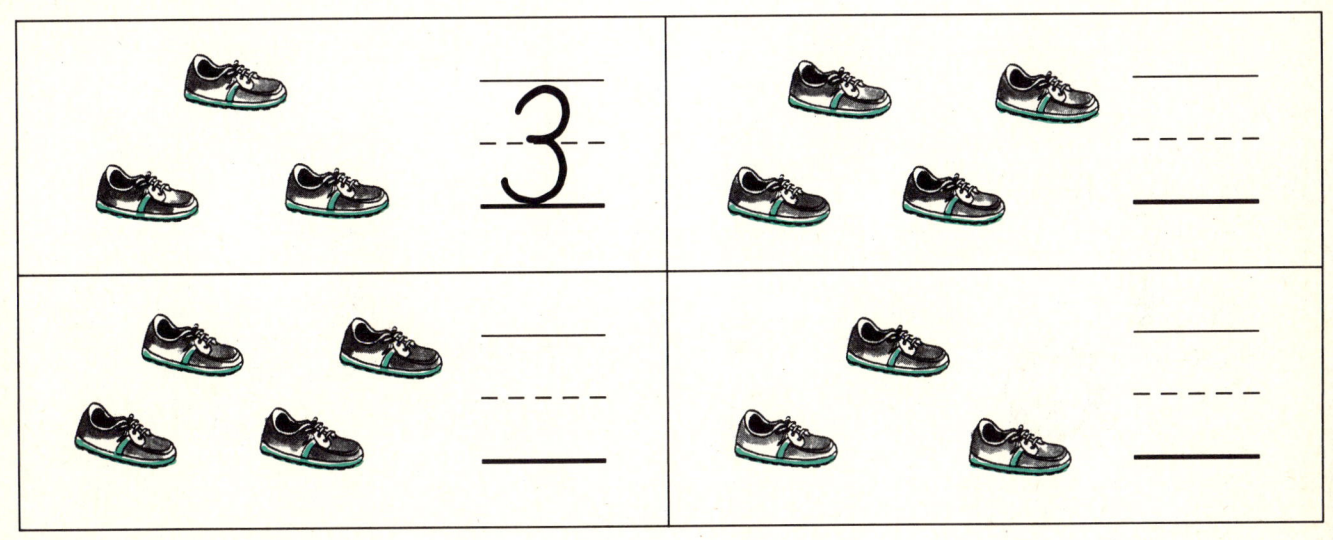

| (3 shoes) 3 | (4 shoes) ___ |
| (4 shoes) ___ | (4 shoes) ___ |

Using Math

◆ This is a [soccer player] .

Write how many. ___

3

Five and Six

How many?

| 5 five | | 6 six | |

Guided Practice

◆ Circle how many.

	⑤ 6		5 6
	5 6		5 6
	5 6		5 6

Practice

◆ **Write 5 and 6.**

5 5 5

6 6

◆ **Write how many.**

6

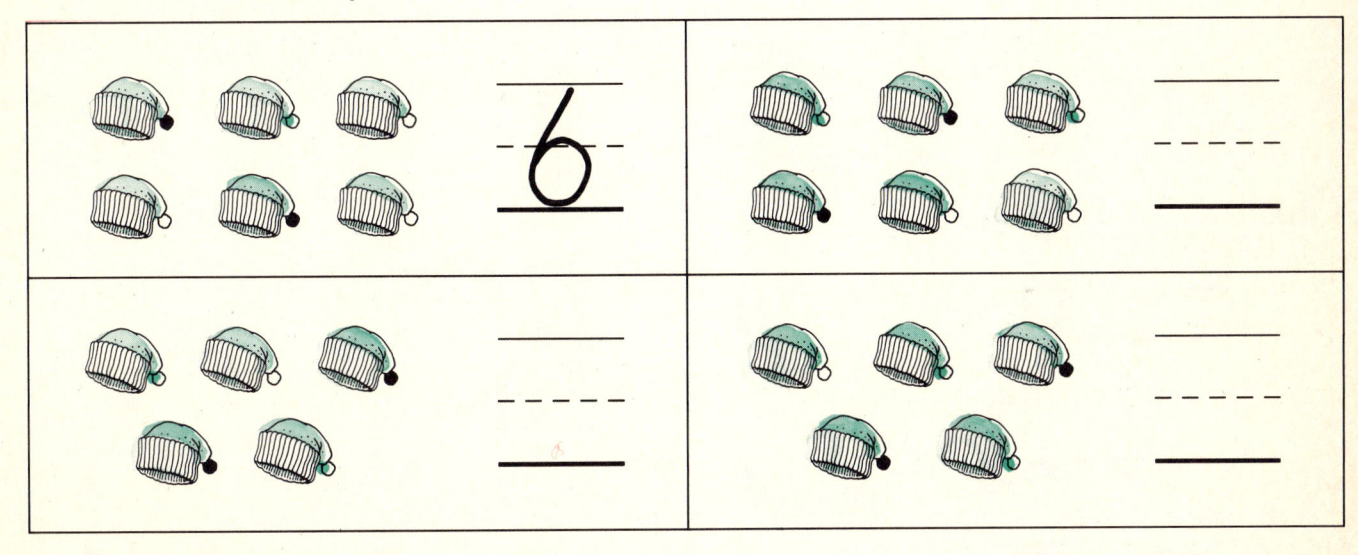

Using Math

◆ This is a ⬤ .

Write how many. _____

7

4

Zero

How many?

| **0** zero | **1** one | **2** two |

Guided Practice

◆ Circle how many.

(0) 1 2

0 1 2

0 1 2

0 1 2

0 1 2

0 1 2

Practice

◆ Write 0.

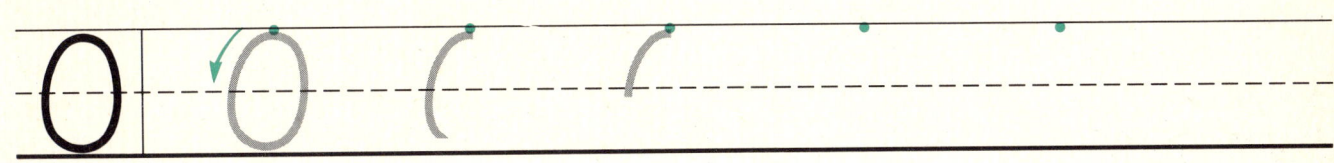

◆ Write how many.

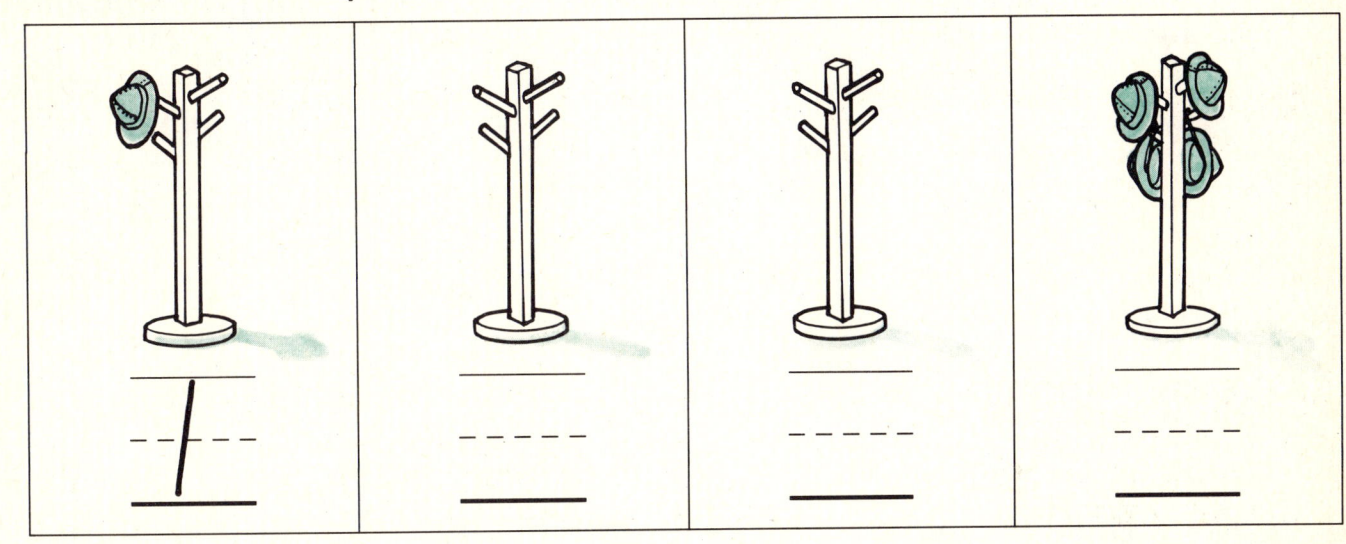

Using Math

◆ This is a 🎩.

Write how many.

5

Seven and Eight

How many?

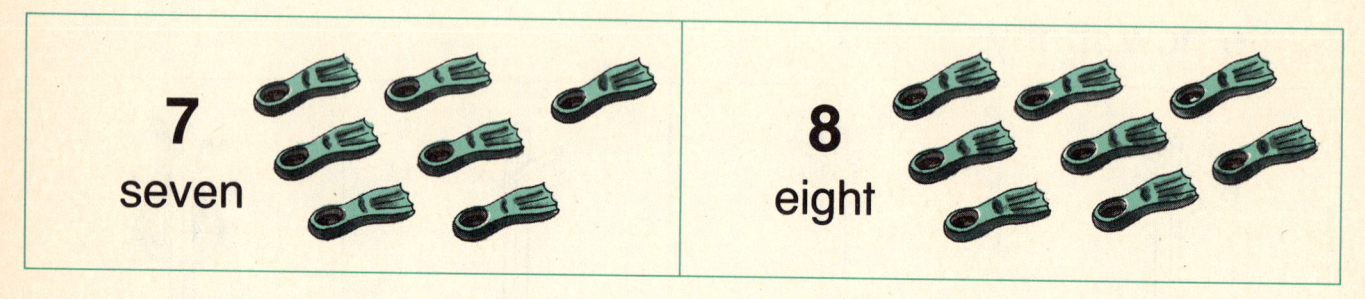

| 7 seven | 8 eight |

Guided Practice

◆ Circle how many.

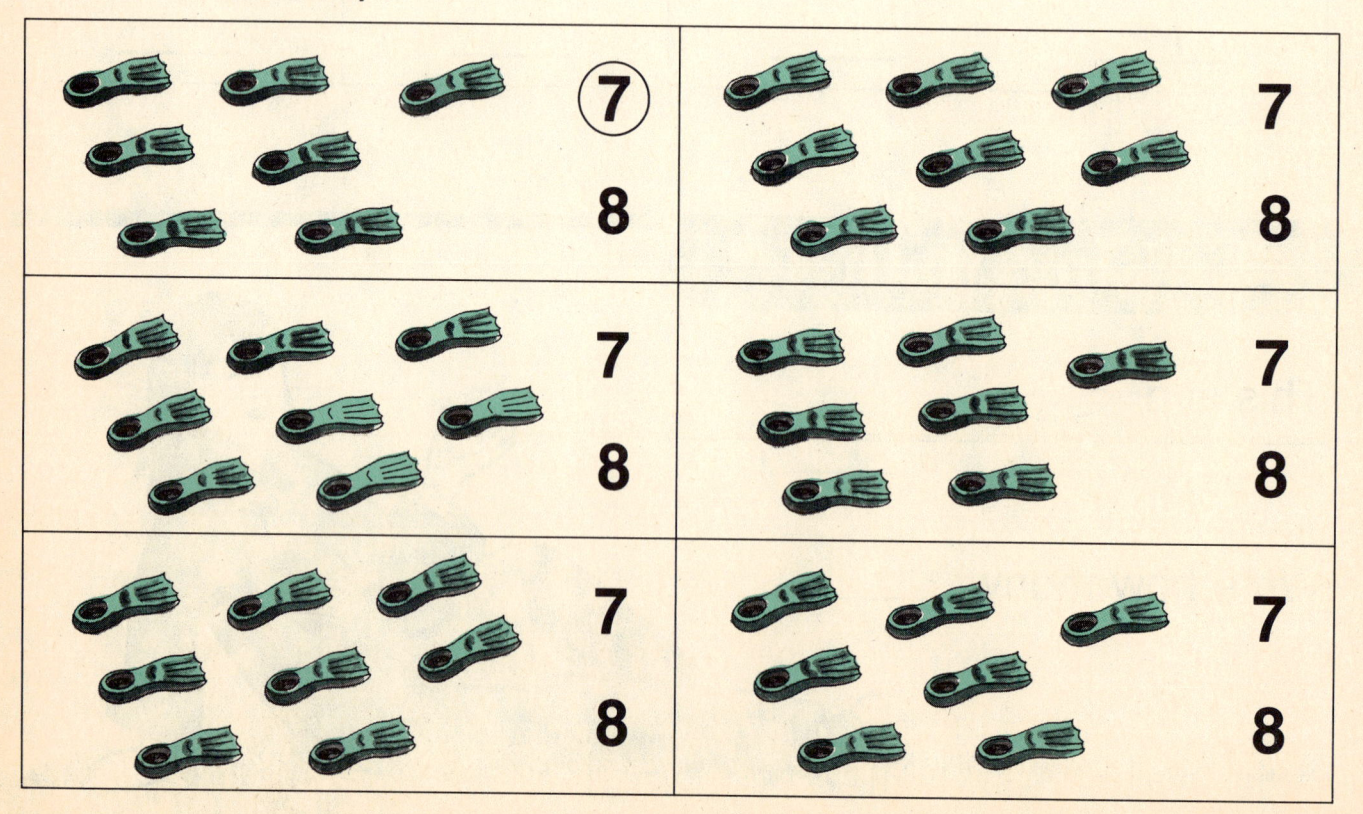

⑦ 8

7 8

7 8

7 8

7 8

7 8

Practice

◆ Write 7 and 8.

7 7 7 7 7 7

8 8 8 8 8

◆ Write how many.

7

___

___ ___

___ ___

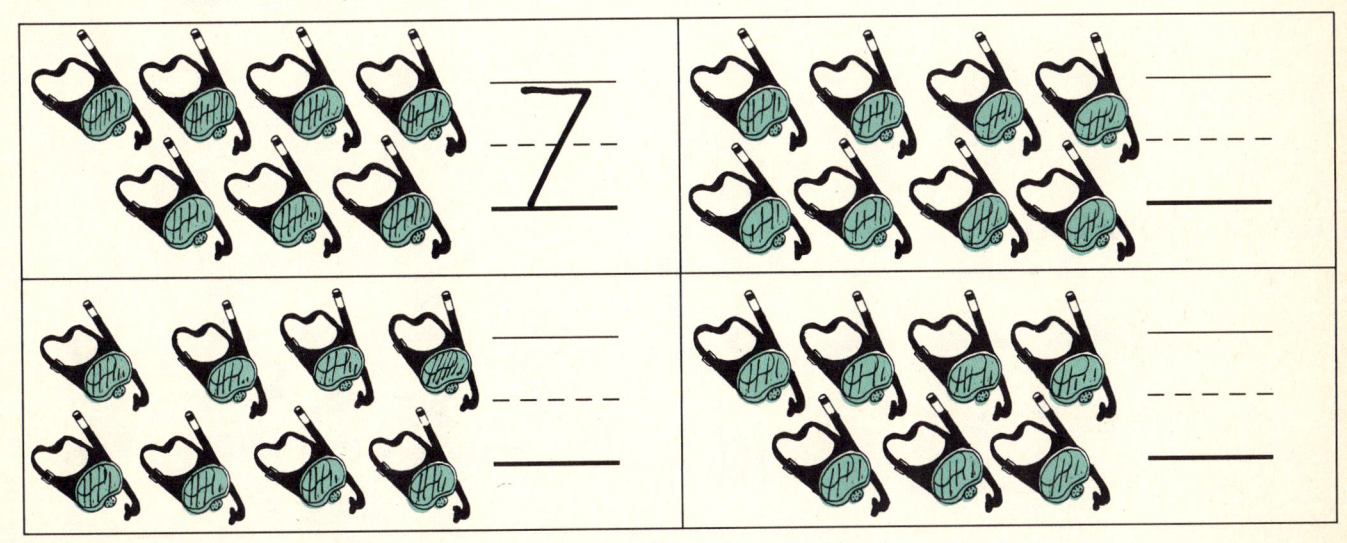

Using Math

◆ This is a 🐟.

___

___

Write how many. ___

6

Nine and Ten

How many?

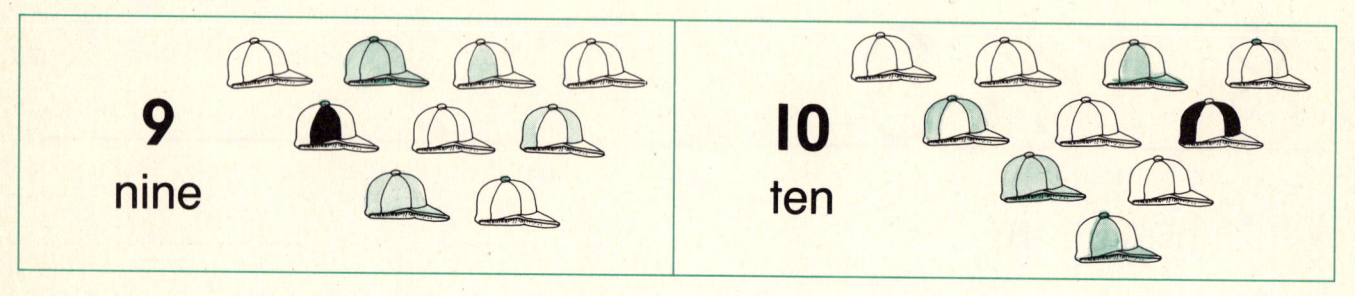

| 9 nine | 10 ten |

Guided Practice

◆ Circle how many.

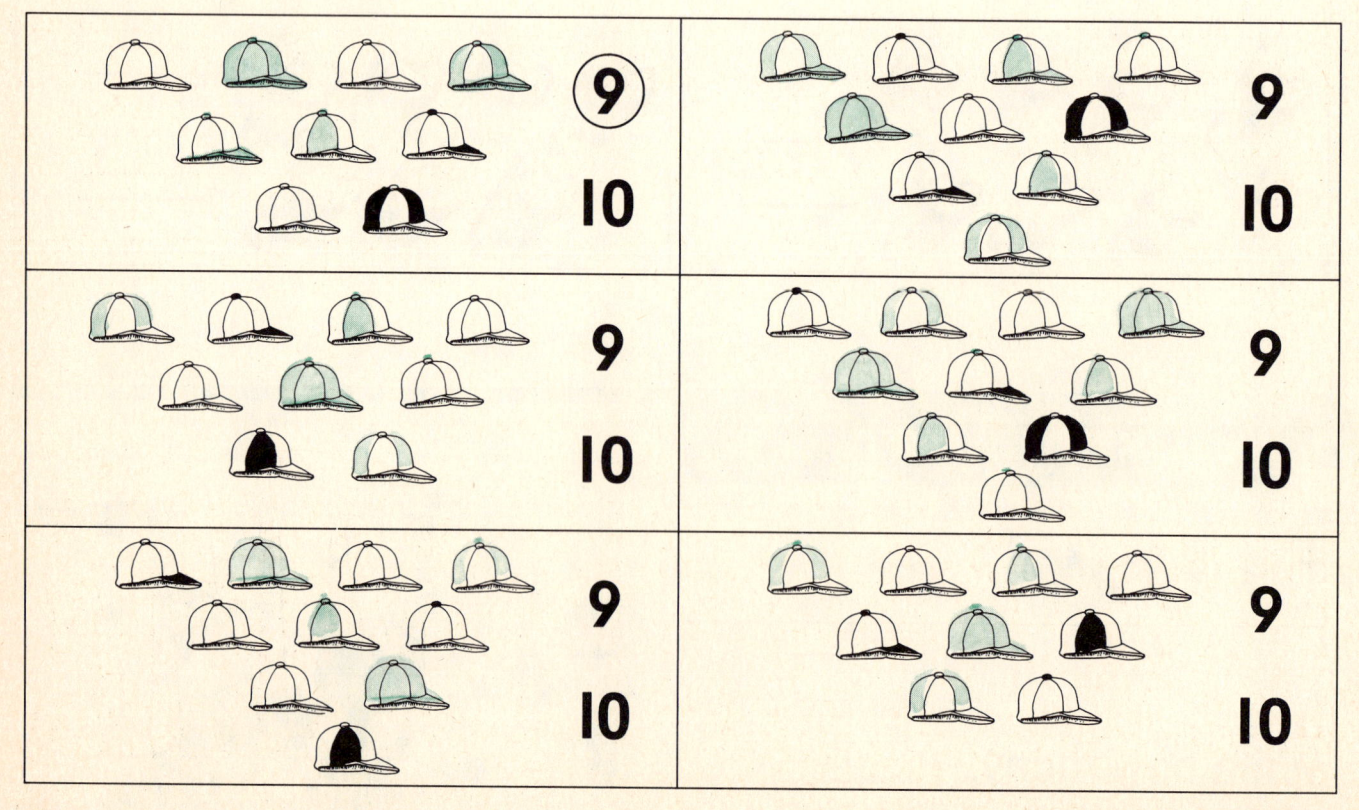

⑨ 10	9 10
9 10	9 10
9 10	9 10

12

Practice

◆ Write 9 and 10.

9 9 9 9

10 10 10 10

◆ Write how many.

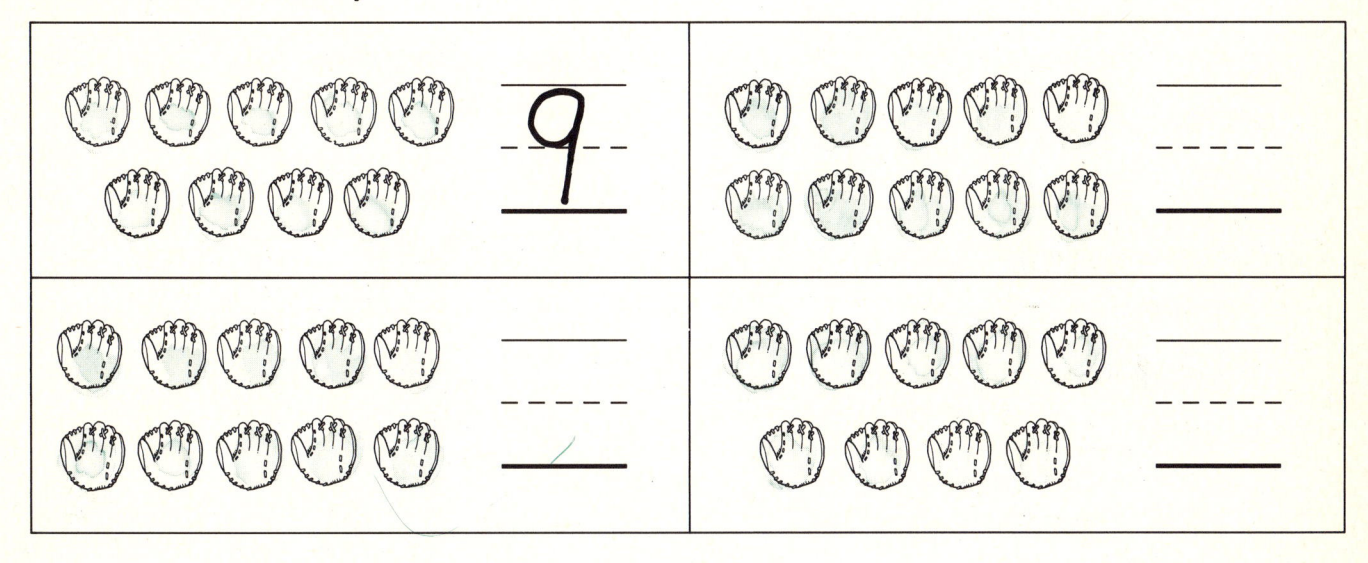

(9 gloves)	9
(10 gloves)	___
(10 gloves)	___
(9 gloves)	___

Using Math

◆ This is a 🏏.

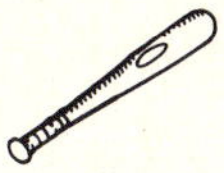

Write how many. ___

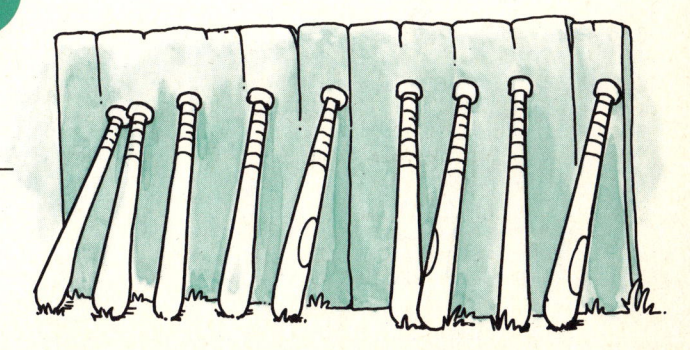

13

7

Pennies

1 penny
1 cent
1¢

1 penny
1 cent
1¢

Guided Practice

◆ How much money?

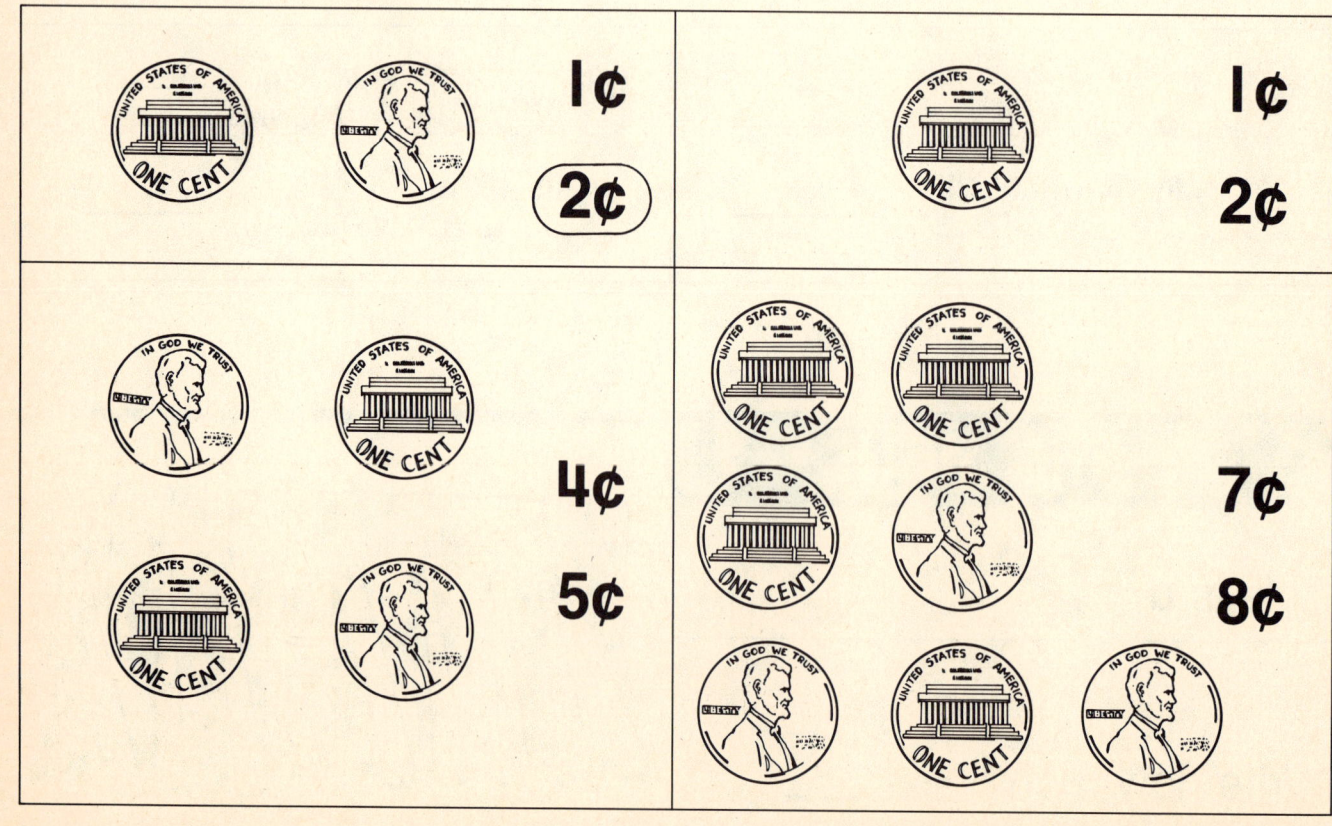

(2 pennies)	1¢ / (2¢)
(1 penny)	1¢ / 2¢
(4 pennies)	4¢ / 5¢
(7 pennies)	7¢ / 8¢

Practice

◆ Write ¢.

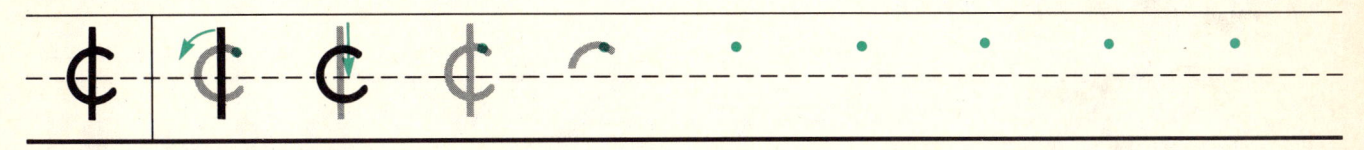

¢ ¢ ¢ ¢

◆ Write how much money.

5¢

Using Math

◆ Ring how much money.

15

Problem Solving 8

Use a Picture

Guided Practice

◆ Count the pictures.
Write how many.

4

Practice

◆ Count the pictures.
Write how many.

Review

◆ Write how many.

pages 2–3

pages 4–5

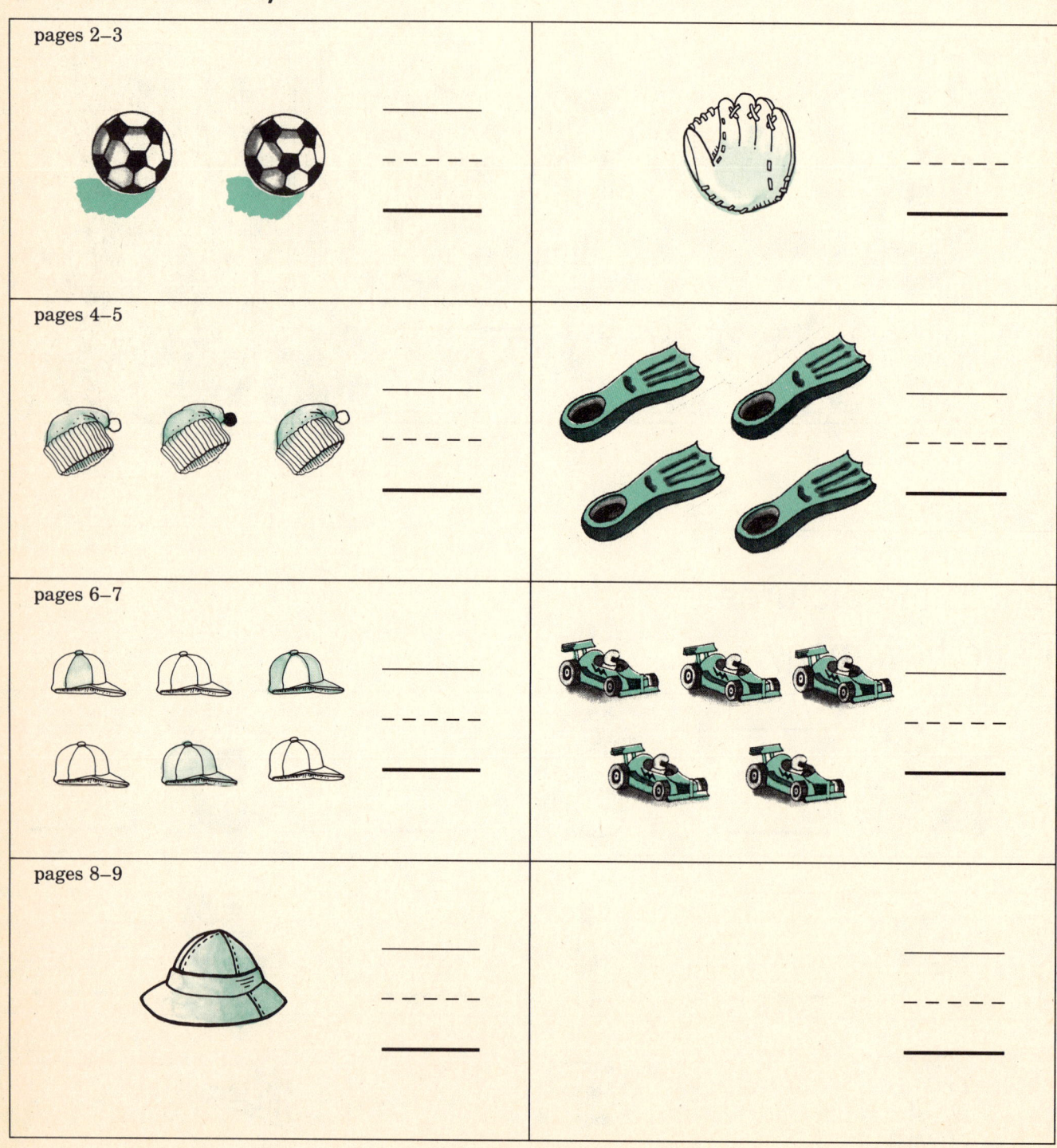

pages 6–7

pages 8–9

18

CHAPTER 1

◆ Write how many.

pages 10–11

pages 12–13

◆ Write how much money. pages 14–15

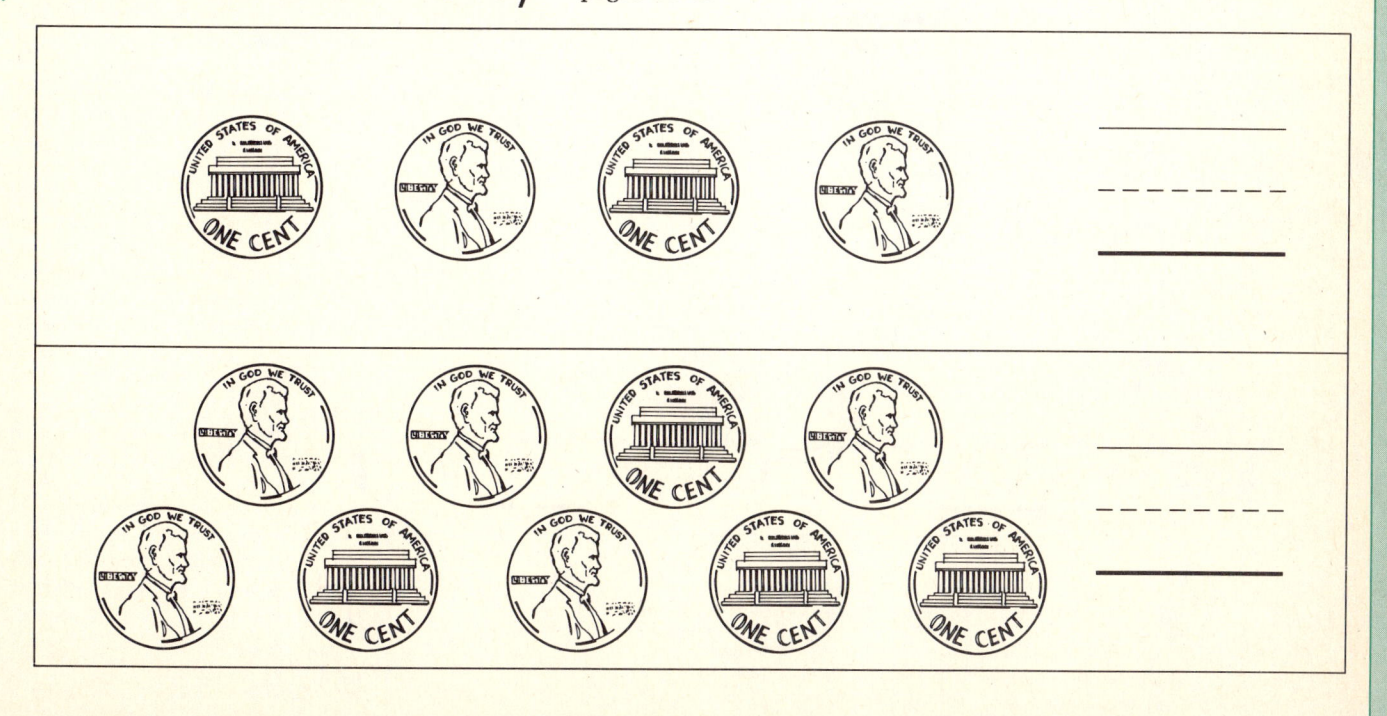

19

Review

CHAPTER 1

◆ Count the animals.
Write how many.

pages 16–17

Test

CHAPTER 1

◆ Write the number.

◆ Write how much money.

Test

CHAPTER 1

◆ Count the pictures.
Write how many.

Name _____

CHAPTER 2

Addition Facts Through 10

Martie is feeding the ducks.
How many ducks stayed in the water?
How many ducks came out of the water?
How many ducks are there in all?

23

1

Adding to 5

How many 🍎 in all?

Add.
   3
+ 2
   5 🍎 in all.

Guided Practice

◆ Add.

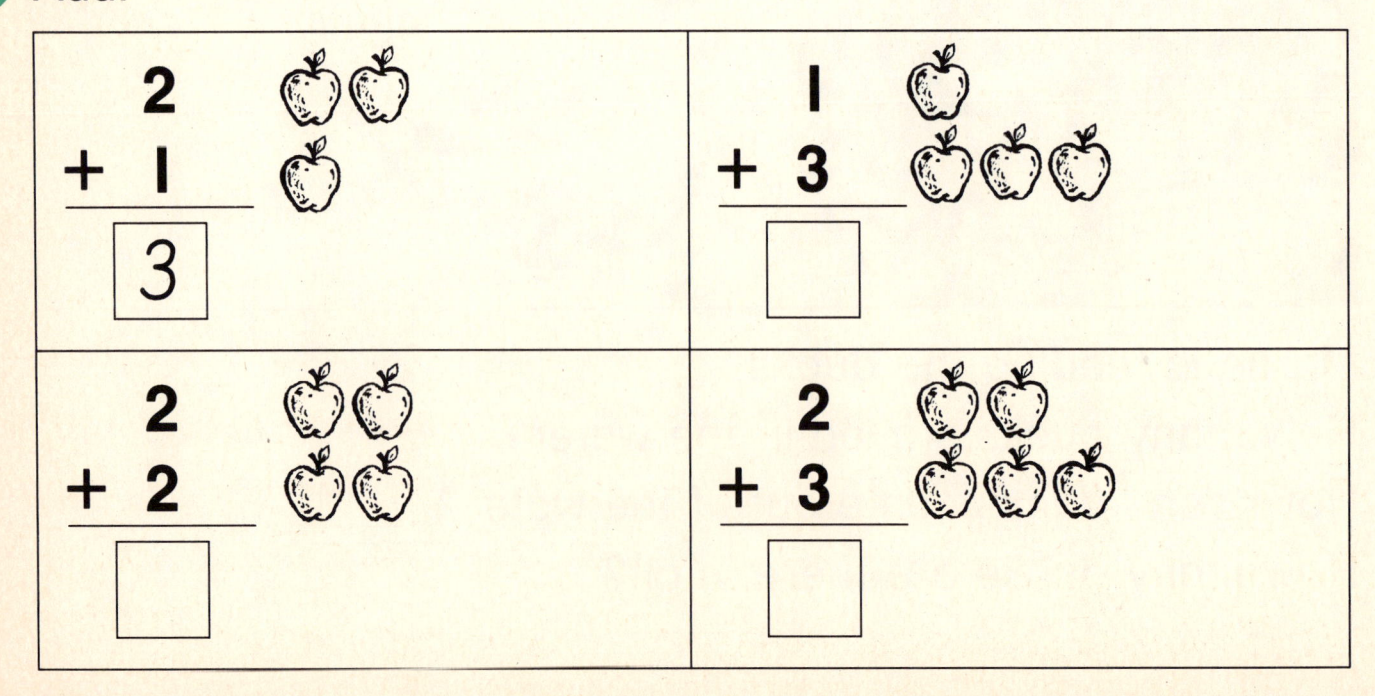

   2
+ 1
   3

   1
+ 3
☐

   2
+ 2
☐

   2
+ 3
☐

24

Practice

◆ Add.

```
  3
+ 1
____
[  ]
```

```
  1
+ 2
____
[  ]
```

```
  2
+ 2
____
[  ]
```

```
  1
+ 1
____
[  ]
```

```
  2
+ 3
____
[  ]
```

```
  1
+ 3
____
[  ]
```

```
  3
+ 1
____
[  ]
```

```
  3
+ 2
____
[  ]
```

```
  2
+ 1
____
[  ]
```

Using Math

◆ How many 🍎 in all?

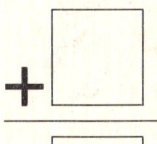

```
  [2]
+ [ ]
____
 [ ]   in all.
```

25

2

Adding to 7

How many 🐕 in all?

Add.
```
  5
+ 2
  7
```
🐕 in all.

Guided Practice

◆ Add.

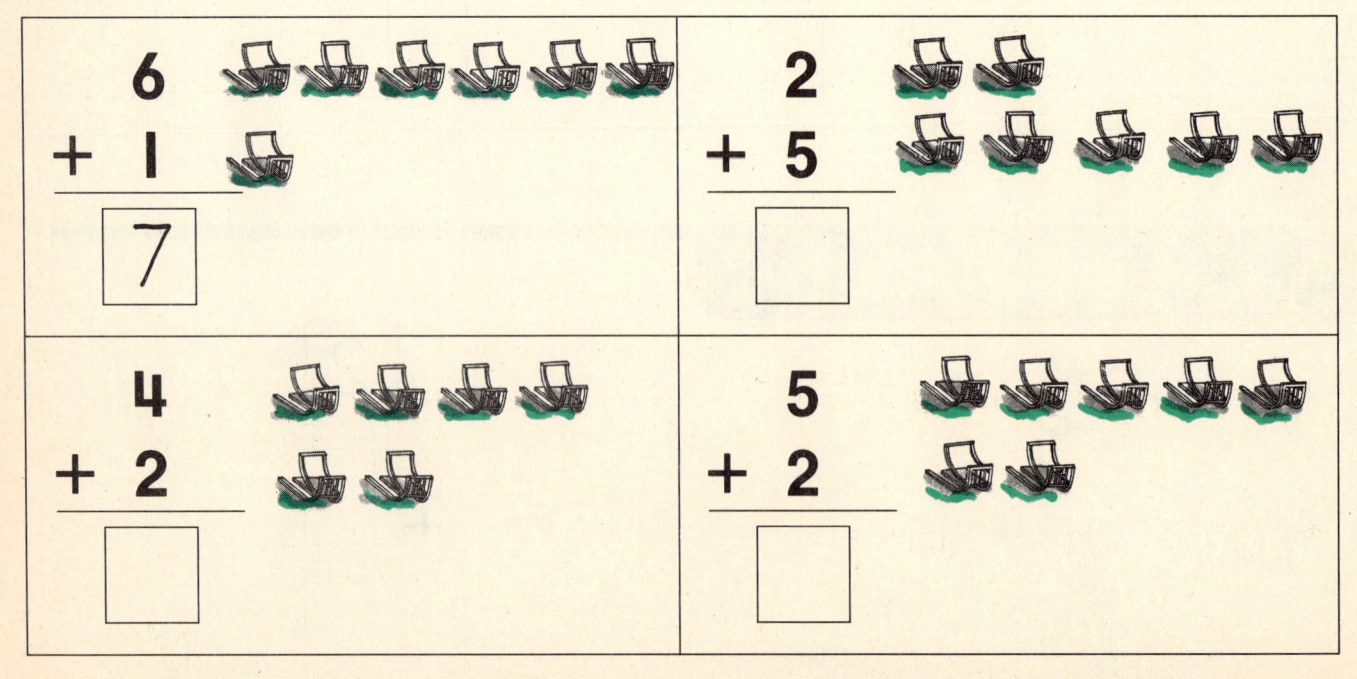

```
  6
+ 1
─────
  7
```

```
  2
+ 5
─────
  ☐
```

```
  4
+ 2
─────
  ☐
```

```
  5
+ 2
─────
  ☐
```

26

Practice

◆ Add.

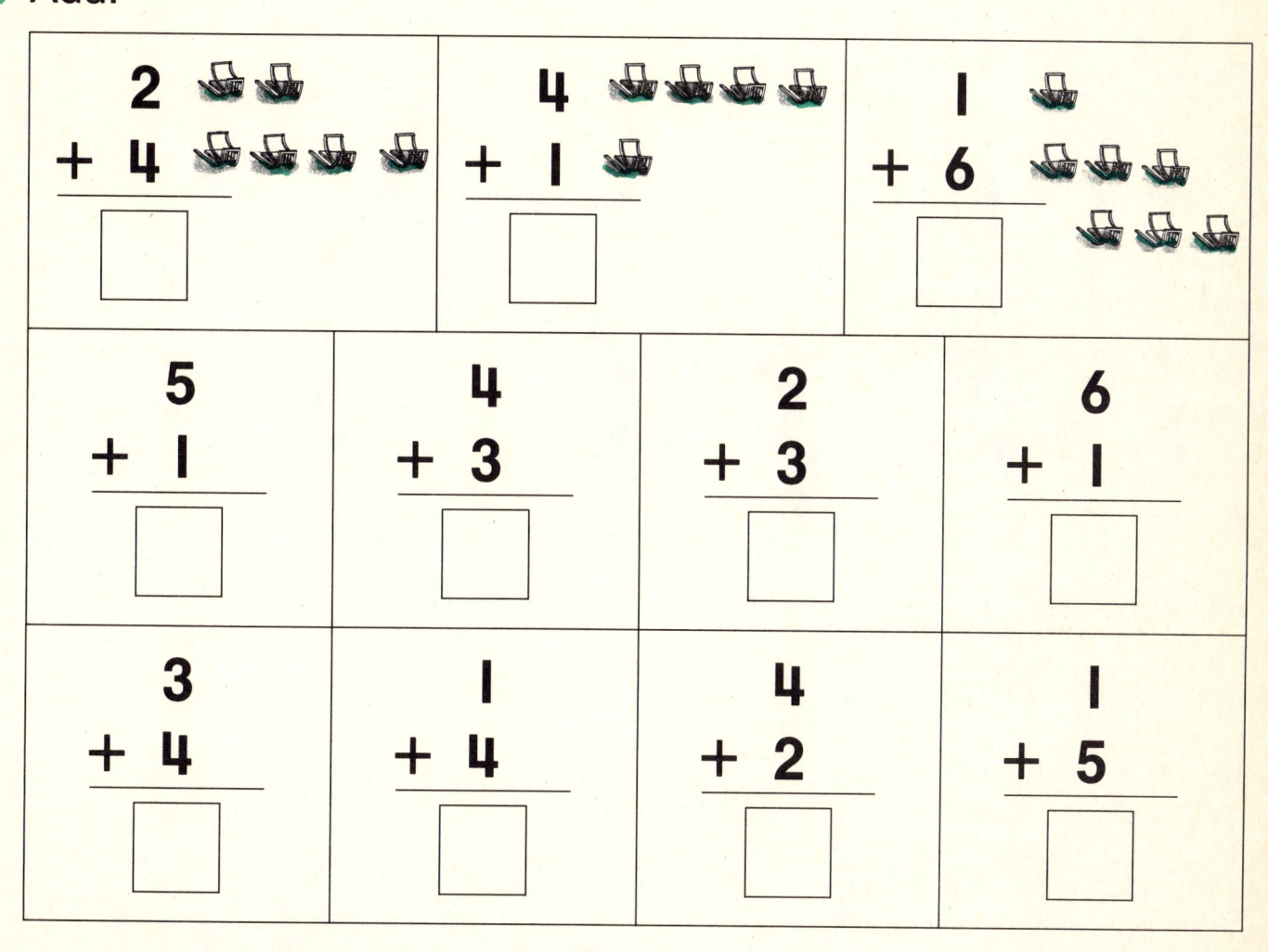

| 2 + 4 = ☐ | 4 + 1 = ☐ | 1 + 6 = ☐ |

| 5 + 1 = ☐ | 4 + 3 = ☐ | 2 + 3 = ☐ | 6 + 1 = ☐ |

| 3 + 4 = ☐ | 1 + 4 = ☐ | 4 + 2 = ☐ | 1 + 5 = ☐ |

Using Math

◆ How many 🐕 in all?

☐ + ☐ = ☐ in all.

27

3

Adding with 0

How many 🐴 in all?

Add.

$$\begin{array}{r} 4 \\ +\ 0 \\ \hline 4 \end{array}$$ 🐴 in all.

Guided Practice

◆ Add.

$$\begin{array}{r} 3 \\ +\ 0 \\ \hline \boxed{3} \end{array}$$

$$\begin{array}{r} 0 \\ +\ 5 \\ \hline \boxed{} \end{array}$$

$$\begin{array}{r} 2 \\ +\ 0 \\ \hline \boxed{} \end{array}$$

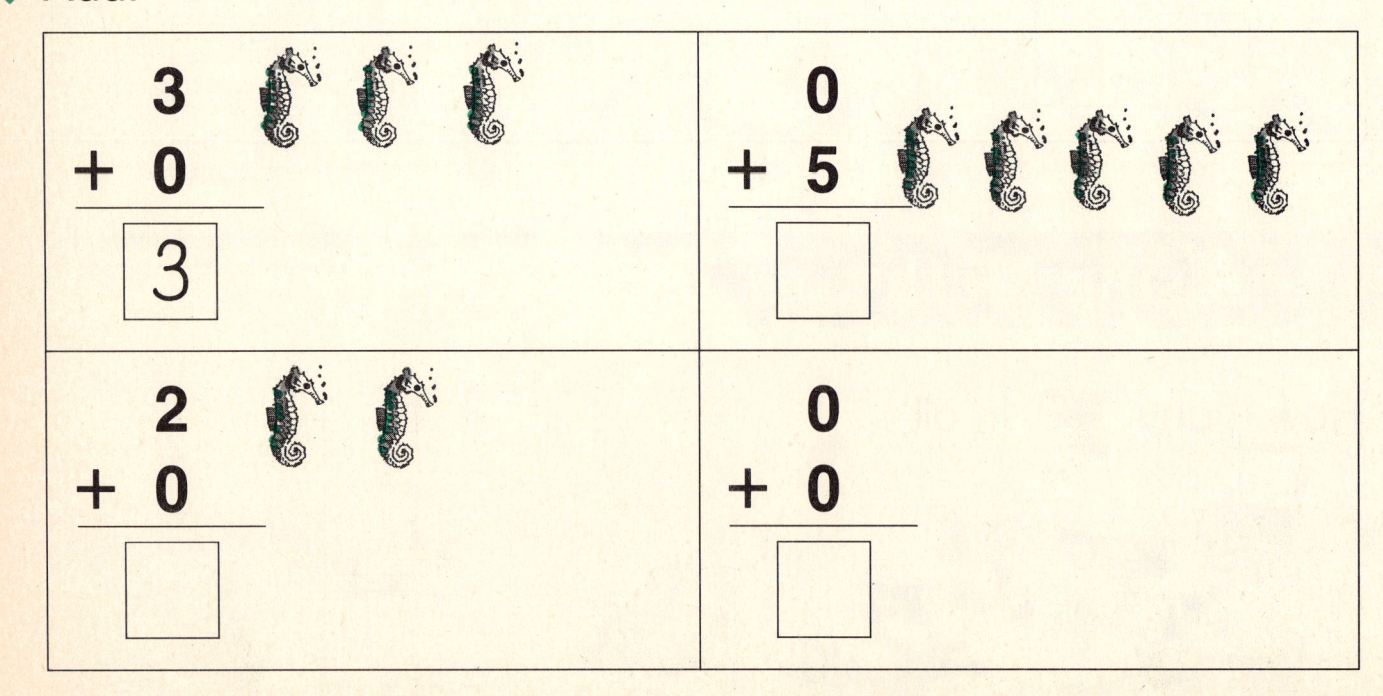

$$\begin{array}{r} 0 \\ +\ 0 \\ \hline \boxed{} \end{array}$$

Practice

◆ Add.

4 + 0  = ☐	0 + 2  = ☐	5 + 0  = ☐

6 + 0 = ☐	5 + 1 = ☐	7 + 0 = ☐	0 + 4 = ☐

0 + 3 = ☐	1 + 2 = ☐	0 + 1 = ☐	0 + 7 = ☐

Using Math

◆ How many 🐠 in all?

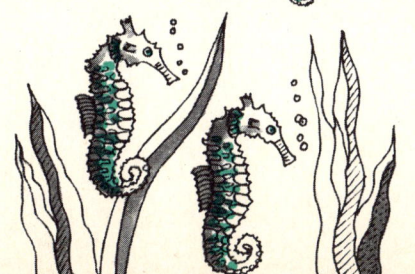

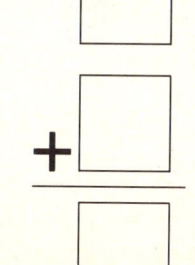

☐ + ☐ = ☐ in all.

29

4

Adding to 8

How many 🐦 in all?

Add.
$$\begin{array}{r}5\\+3\\\hline 8\end{array}$$
↑
sum

🐦 in all.

Guided Practice

◆ Add.

$$\begin{array}{r}1\\+7\\\hline \boxed{8}\end{array}$$

$$\begin{array}{r}3\\+5\\\hline \boxed{}\end{array}$$

$$\begin{array}{r}8\\+0\\\hline \boxed{}\end{array}$$

$$\begin{array}{r}2\\+6\\\hline \boxed{}\end{array}$$

Practice

◆ Add.

7 + 1 ───	4 + 3 ───	6 + 2 ───
4 + 4 ───	0 + 8 ───	1 + 6 ───	1 + 7 ───
7 + 0 ───	5 + 3 ───	4 + 2 ───	2 + 6 ───

Using Math

◆ How many 🐦 in all?

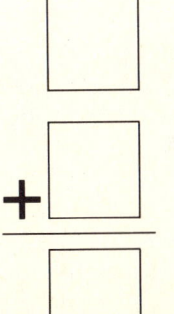

☐
+ ☐
───
☐   in all.

31

5

Adding to 9

How many ☐ in all?

Add.
  4
+ 5
―――
  9 ☐ in all.

Guided Practice

◆ Add.

```
   3  ☐☐☐
+  6  ☐☐☐☐☐☐
―――
   [9]
```

```
   2  ☐☐
+  7  ☐☐☐☐☐☐☐
―――
   [ ]
```

```
   8  ☐☐☐☐☐☐☐☐
+  1  ☐
―――
   [ ]
```

```
   9  ☐☐☐☐☐☐☐☐☐
+  0
―――
   [ ]
```

32

Practice

◆ Add.

5 ▢▢▢▢▢ + 4 ▢▢▢▢ ☐	4 ▢▢▢▢ + 3 ▢▢▢ ☐	6 ▢▢▢▢▢▢ + 3 ▢▢▢ ☐

7 + 2 ☐	1 + 7 ☐	0 + 9 ☐	3 + 6 ☐
1 + 8 ☐	2 + 5 ☐	4 + 5 ☐	2 + 7 ☐

Using Math

◆ How many ☐ in all?

☐
+ ☐
—
☐ in all.

33

6

Adding to 10

How many 🌷 in all?

Add.
```
   2
 + 8
 ----
  10
```
🌷 in all.

Guided Practice

◆ Add.

```
   8
 + 2
 ----
  10
```

```
   6
 + 4
 ----
```

```
   4
 + 6
 ----
```

```
   7
 + 3
 ----
```

Practice

◆ Add.

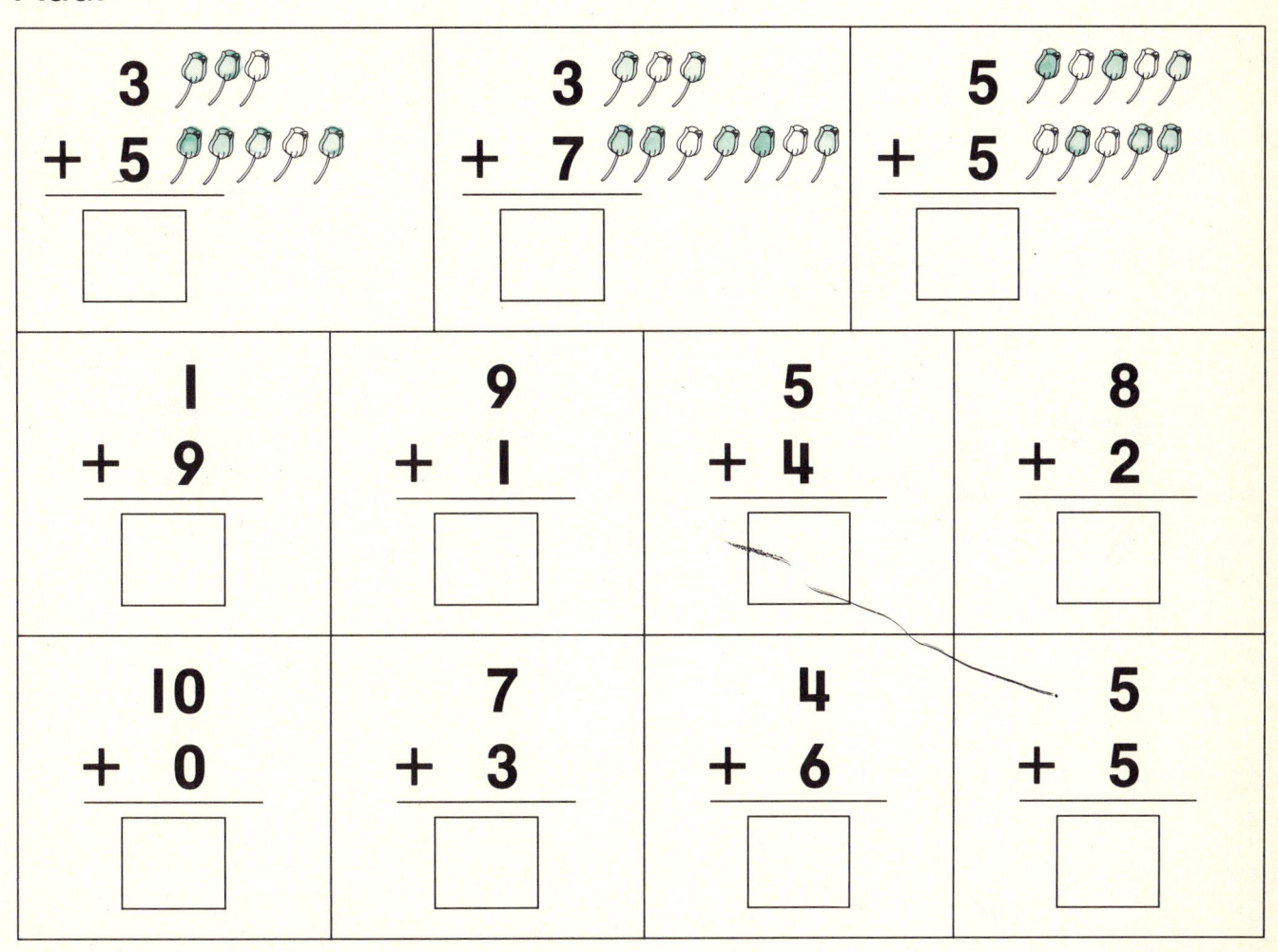

| 3 + 5 = ☐ | 3 + 7 = ☐ | 5 + 5 = ☐ |

| 1 + 9 = ☐ | 9 + 1 = ☐ | 5 + 4 = ☐ | 8 + 2 = ☐ |

| 10 + 0 = ☐ | 7 + 3 = ☐ | 4 + 6 = ☐ | 5 + 5 = ☐ |

Problem Solving

◆ Count the pictures.
Write how many.

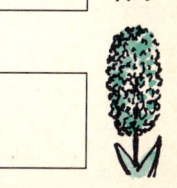

35

7

Nickels

1 nickel
5 cents
5¢

1 nickel
5 cents
5¢

equals

Guided Practice

◆ How much money?

8¢
9¢

5¢
6¢

3¢
5¢

5¢
6¢

Practice

◆ Write how much money.

Using Math

◆ Ring how much money.

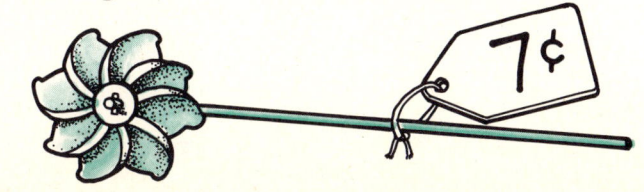

7¢

Problem Solving 8

Use a Picture

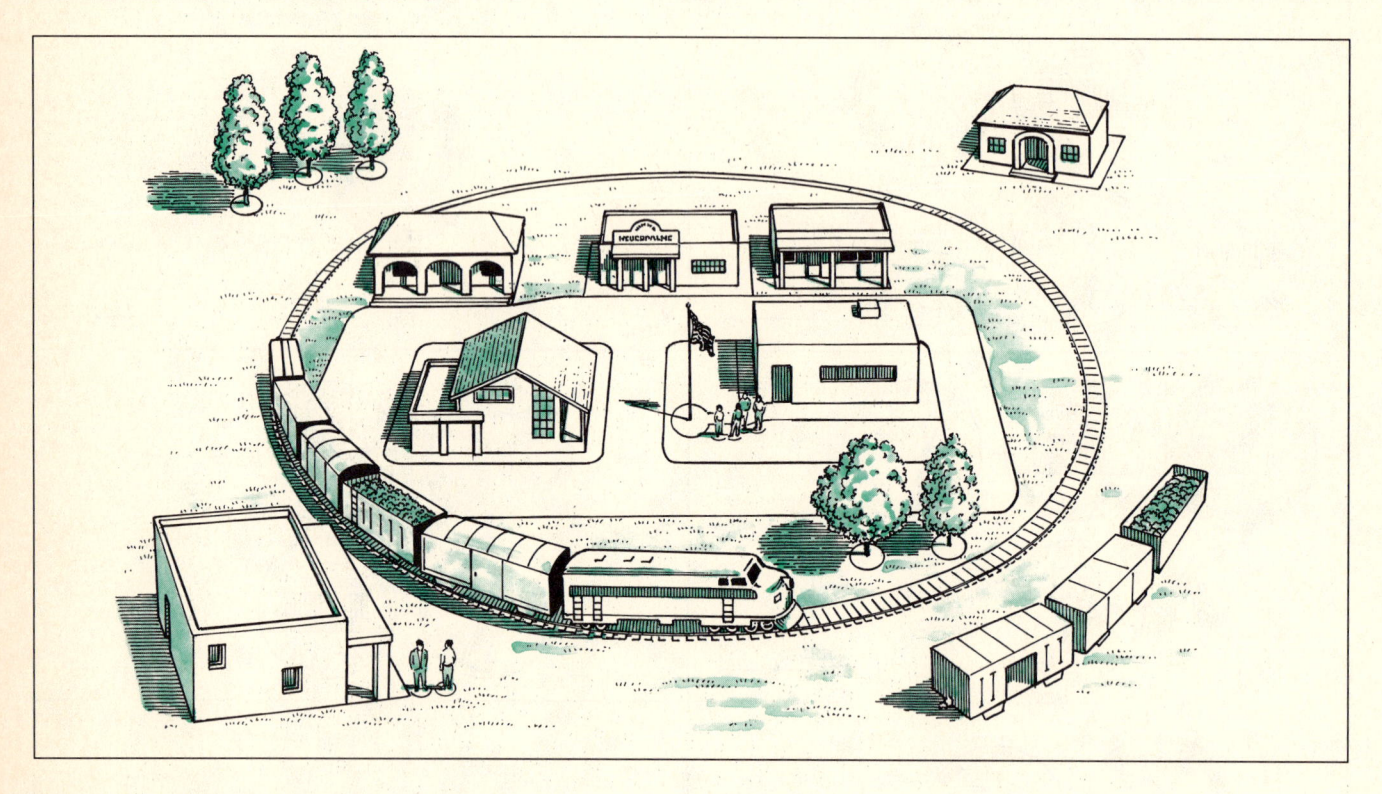

Guided Practice

◆ Look at the picture.
Write how many. Add.

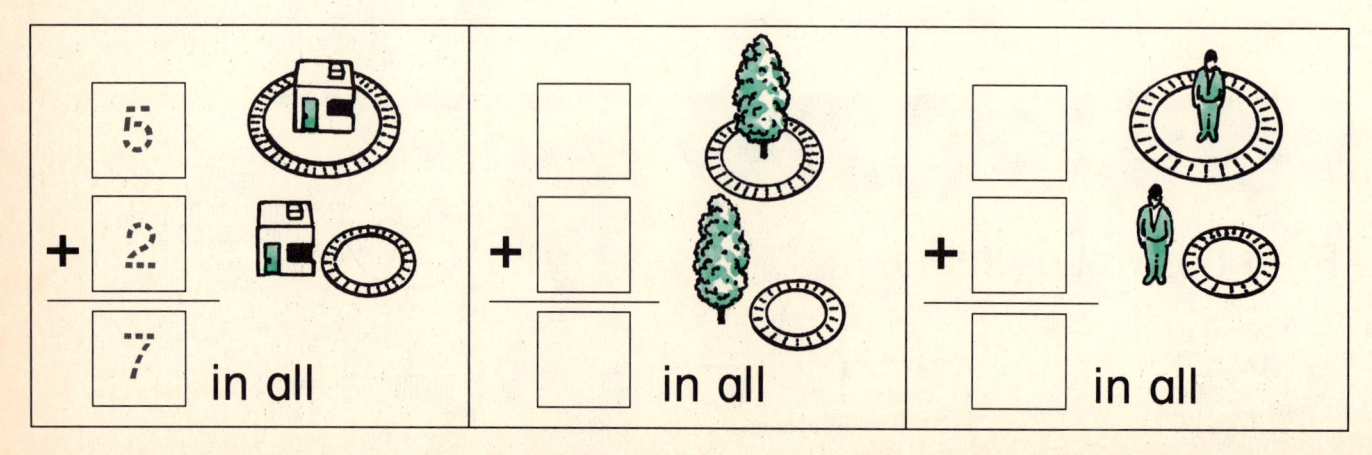

```
  5
+ 2
  7  in all
```

```
+ __
  __   in all
```

```
+ __
  __   in all
```

38

Practice

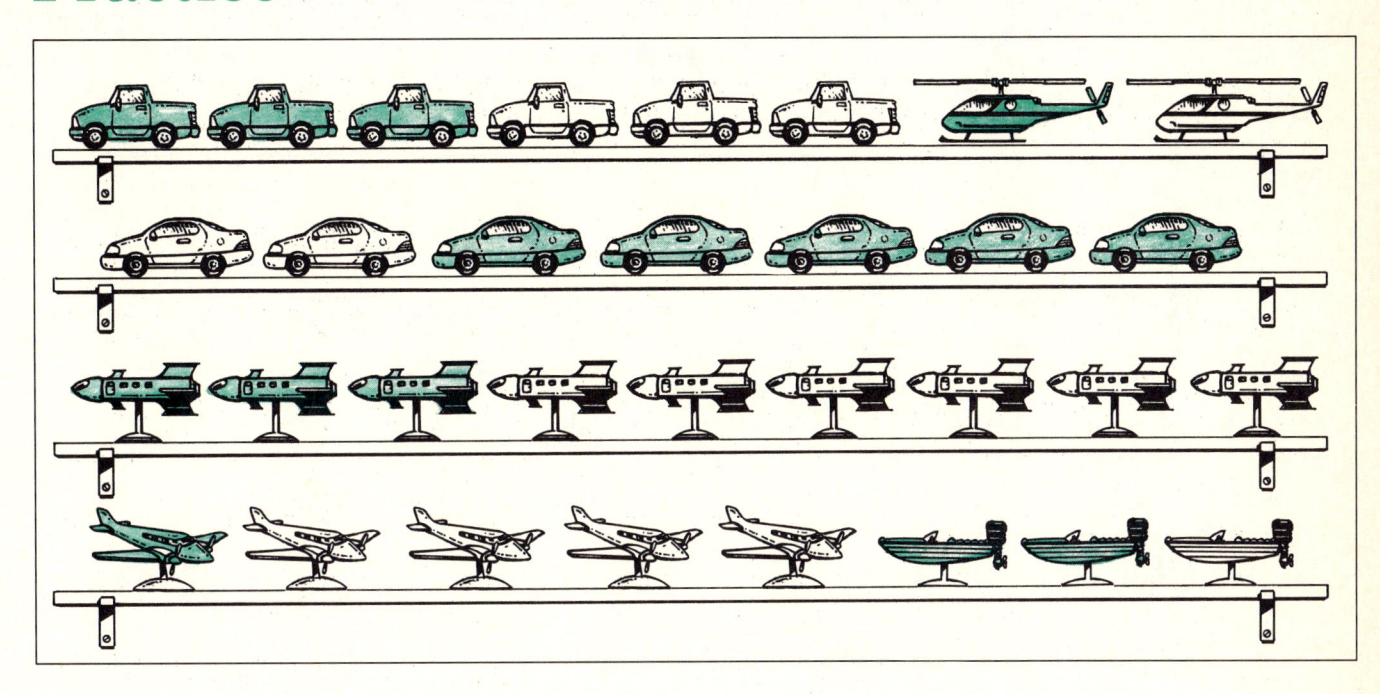

◆ Look at the picture.
Write how many. Add.

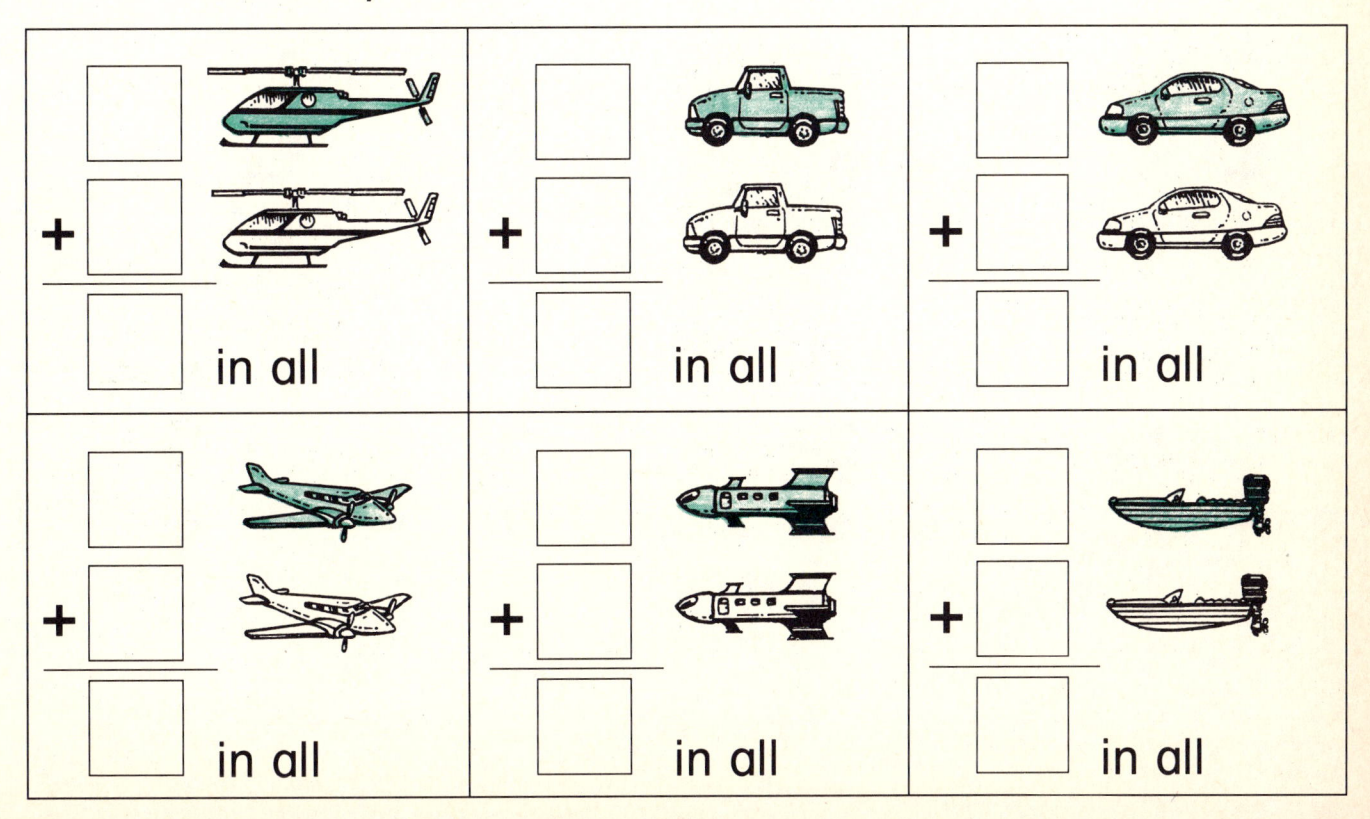

in all

in all

in all

in all

in all

in all

Review

◆ Add.

pages 24–25

```
  1        2        2        1
+ 3      + 3      + 1      + 1
___      ___      ___      ___
[ ]      [ ]      [ ]      [ ]
```

pages 26–27

```
  4        5        5        3
+ 3      + 2      + 1      + 3
___      ___      ___      ___
[ ]      [ ]      [ ]      [ ]
```

pages 28–29

```
  0        5        6        0
+ 1      + 0      + 0      + 4
___      ___      ___      ___
[ ]      [ ]      [ ]      [ ]
```

pages 30–31

```
  2        3        3        4
+ 6      + 5      + 4      + 4
___      ___      ___      ___
[ ]      [ ]      [ ]      [ ]
```

CHAPTER 2

◆ Add.

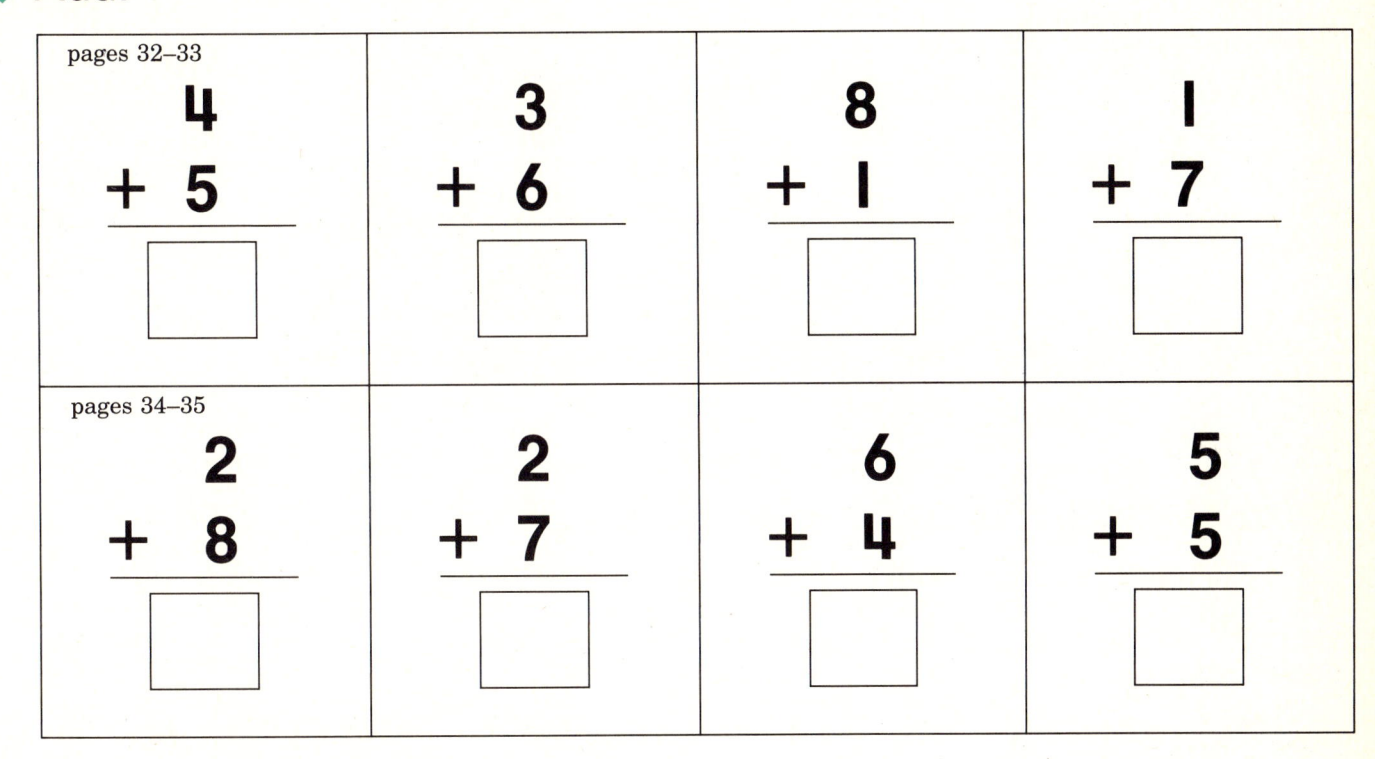

pages 32–33

| 4 | 3 | 8 | 1 |
|+5 | +6 | +1 | +7 |

pages 34–35

| 2 | 2 | 6 | 5 |
|+8 | +7 | +4 | +5 |

◆ How much money?

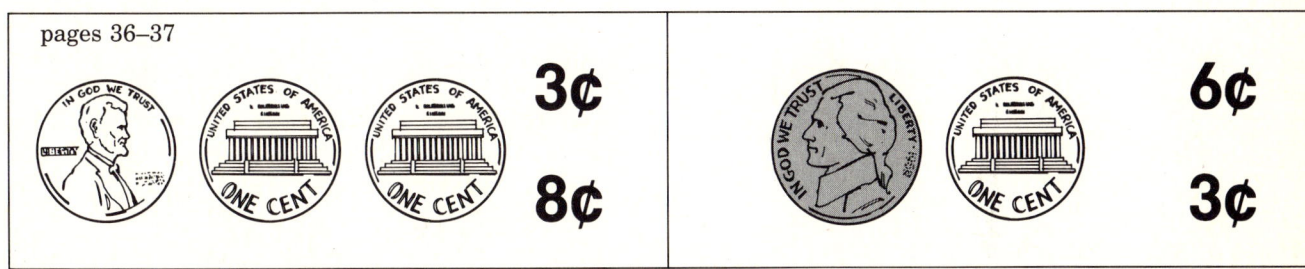

pages 36–37

3¢
8¢

6¢
3¢

◆ Write how much money.

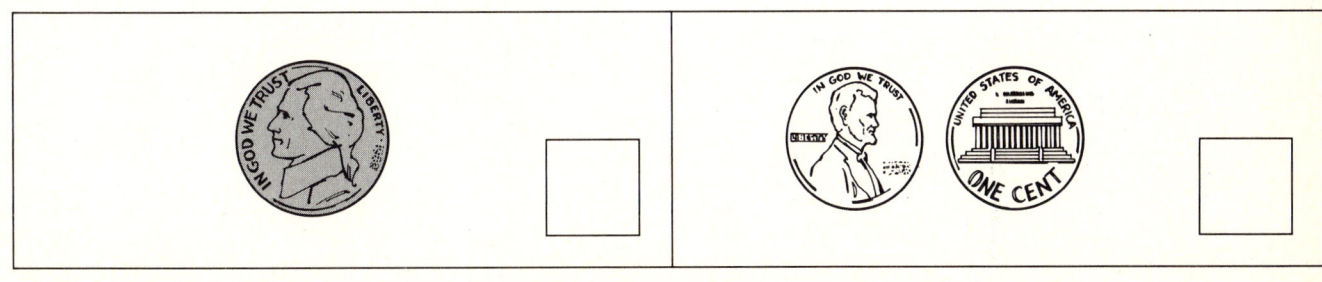

Review

CHAPTER 2

◆ Look at the picture.
Write how many. Add.
pages 38–39

Test

CHAPTER 2

◆ Add.

1 + 2 = ☐	2 + 3 = ☐	3 + 4 = ☐	5 + 1 = ☐
2 + 0 = ☐	0 + 4 = ☐	4 + 4 = ☐	2 + 5 = ☐
7 + 2 = ☐	5 + 3 = ☐	5 + 5 = ☐	4 + 6 = ☐

◆ Write how much money.

Test

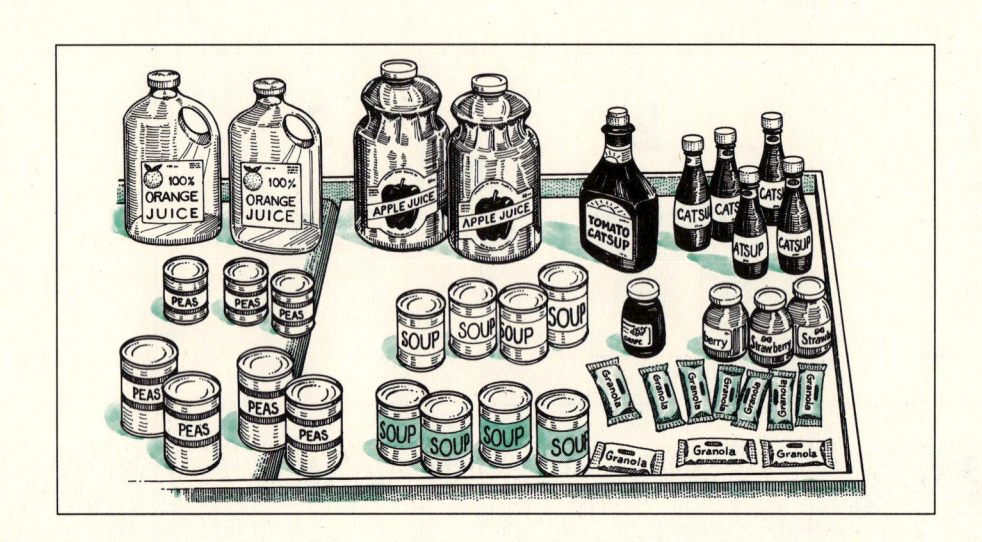

CHAPTER 2

◆ Look at the picture.
Write how many. Add.

☐ + ☐ = ☐ in all	☐ + ☐ = ☐ in all	☐ + ☐ = ☐ in all
☐ + ☐ = ☐ in all	☐ + ☐ = ☐ in all	☐ + ☐ = ☐ in all

44

Name _____

CHAPTER 3

Subtraction Facts Through 10

Shannon has three dogs.
How many dogs do you see?
The other dogs are at home.
How many dogs are at home?

45

1

Subtracting from 2, 3, 4, and 5

How many 🦜 are left?

| 3 | − 1 | 2 |

Subtract.

3
− 1
―――
2   🦜 are left.

Guided Practice

◆ Subtract.

4
− 3
―――
☐ 1

5
− 2
―――
☐

5
− 1
―――
☐

3
− 2
―――
☐

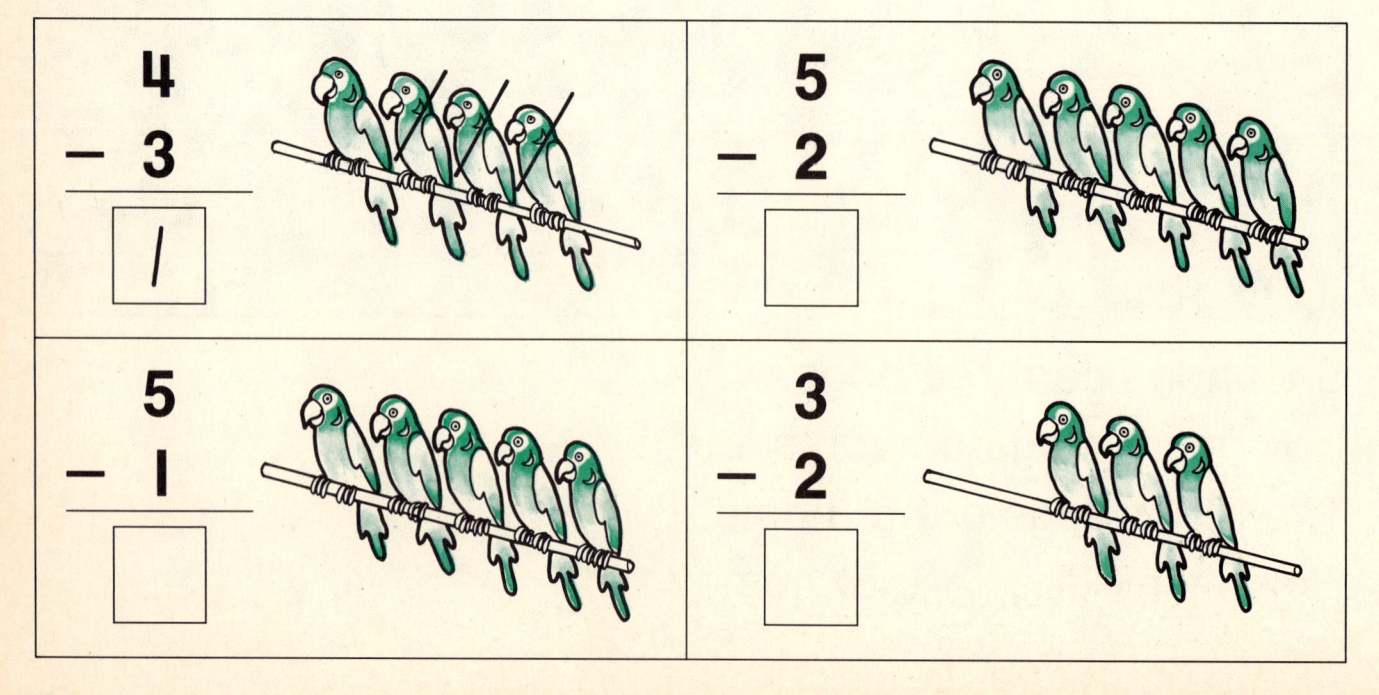

46

Practice

◆ Subtract.

| 4 − 1 = ☐ | 5 − 3 = ☐ | 4 − 2 = ☐ |

| 5 − 5 = ☐ | 2 − 1 = ☐ | 5 − 4 = ☐ | 4 − 3 = ☐ |

| 1 − 1 = ☐ | 3 − 1 = ☐ | 4 − 3 = ☐ | 5 − 1 = ☐ |

Using Math

◆ How many 🐦 are left?

☐ − ☐ = ☐ 🐦 are left.

47

2

Subtracting from 6 and 7

How many 🦋 are left?

| 6 | − 3 | 3 | Subtract.
  6
− 3
―――
  3   🦋 are left. |

Guided Practice

◆ Subtract.

  7
− 4
―――
  [3]

  6
− 6
―――
  [ ]

  7
− 5
―――
  [ ]

  7
− 1
―――
  [ ]

48

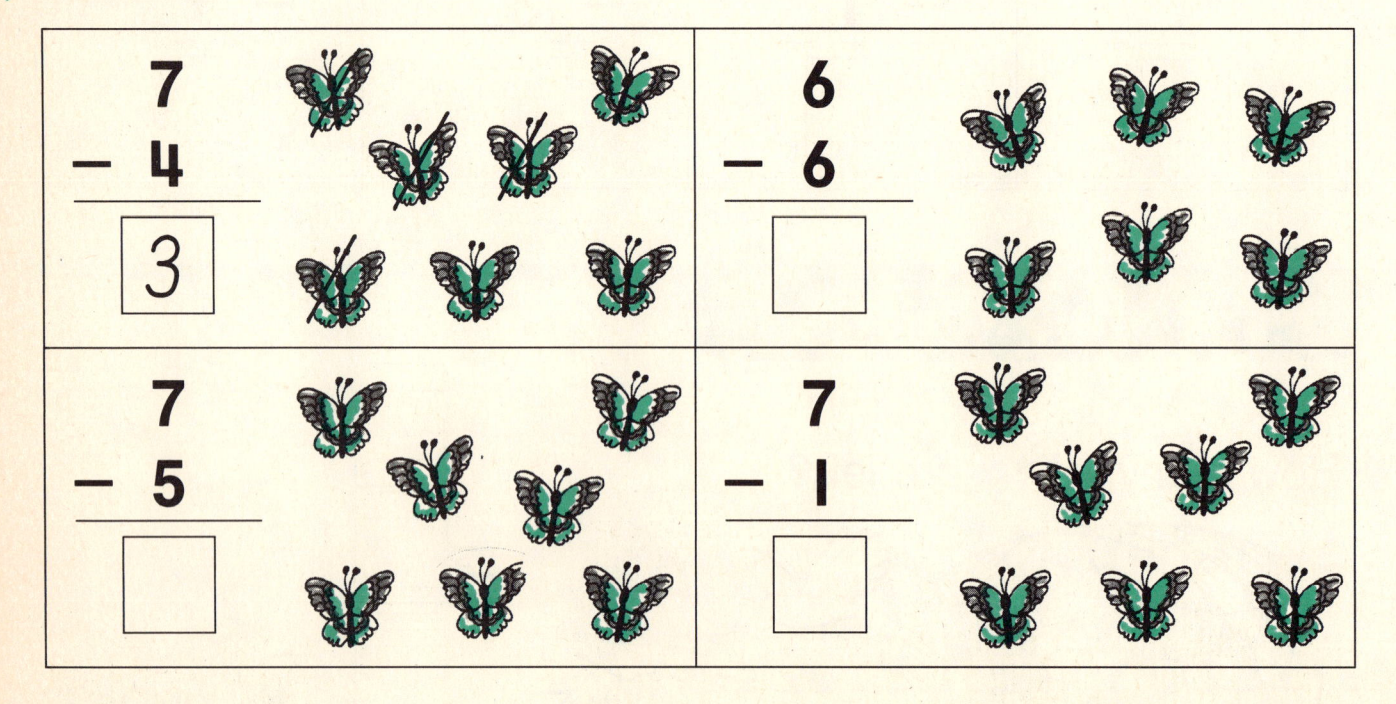

Practice

◆ Subtract.

6 − 4 = ☐	7 − 7 = ☐	6 − 3 = ☐

7 − 3 = ☐	5 − 4 = ☐	7 − 6 = ☐	7 − 2 = ☐

6 − 5 = ☐	6 − 2 = ☐	6 − 1 = ☐	7 − 4 = ☐

Using Math

◆ How many 🦋 are left?

☐ − ☐ = ☐ are left.

49

3

Subtracting 0

How many 🕷 are left?

| 4 | − 0 | 4 |

Subtract.
$$\begin{array}{r}4\\-0\\\hline 4\end{array}$$
🕷 are left.

Guided Practice

◆ Subtract.

$$\begin{array}{r}6\\-0\\\hline 6\end{array}$$

$$\begin{array}{r}1\\-0\\\hline \end{array}$$

$$\begin{array}{r}4\\-0\\\hline \end{array}$$

$$\begin{array}{r}2\\-0\\\hline \end{array}$$

Practice

◆ Subtract.

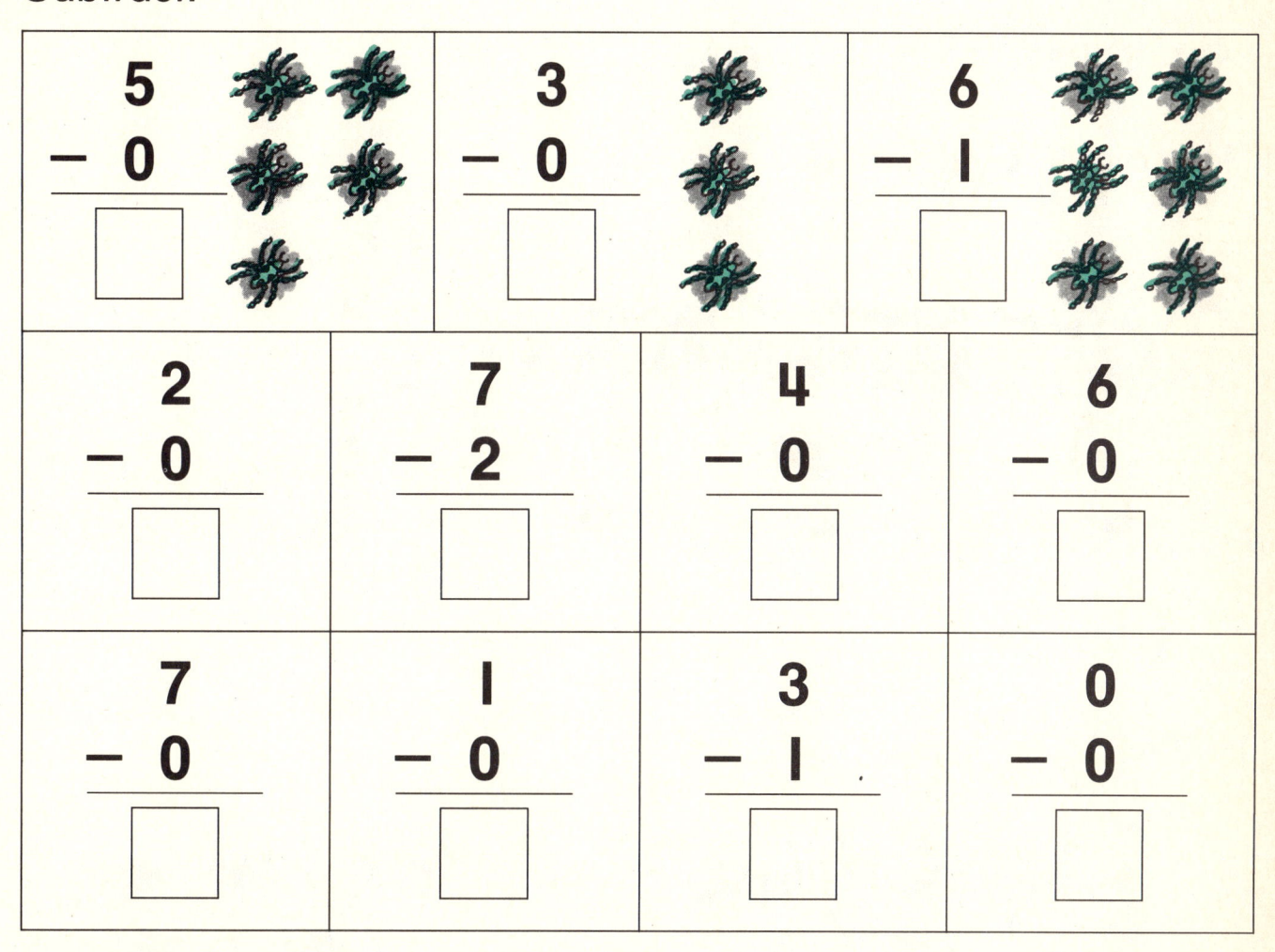

5 − 0 = ☐	3 − 0 = ☐	6 − 1 = ☐
2 − 0 = ☐	7 − 2 = ☐	4 − 0 = ☐	6 − 0 = ☐
7 − 0 = ☐	1 − 0 = ☐	3 − 1 = ☐	0 − 0 = ☐

Using Math

◆ How many 🕷 are left?

☐ − ☐ = ☐ 🕷 are left.

4

Subtracting from 8

How many 🐀 are left?

			Subtract. 8 − 2 ――― 6 🐀 are left. ↑ difference
8	− 2	6	

Guided Practice

◆ Subtract.

8
− 6
―――
2

8
− 3
―――
☐

8
− 8
―――
☐

8
− 0
―――
☐

52

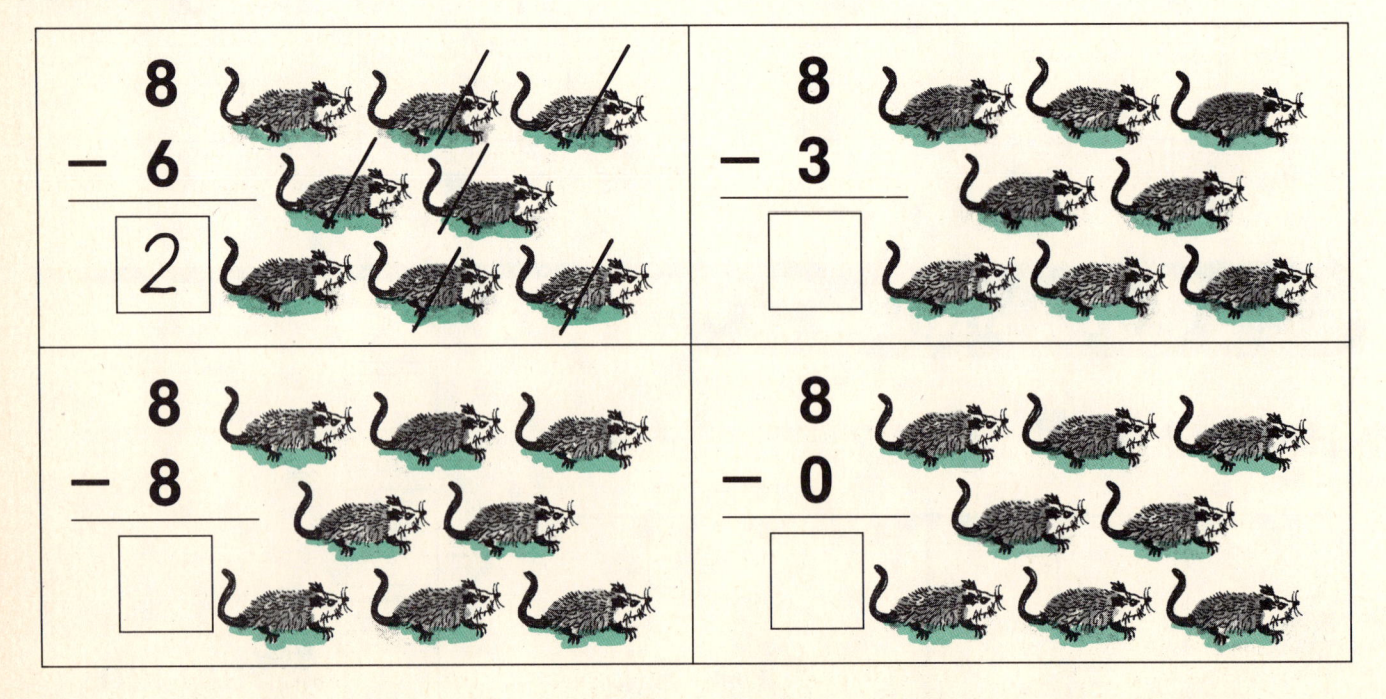

Practice

◆ **Subtract.**

| 8 − 7 = ☐ | 8 − 4 = ☐ | 8 − 5 = ☐ |

| 5 − 3 = ☐ | 8 − 2 = ☐ | 8 − 0 = ☐ | 8 − 6 = ☐ |

| 8 − 8 = ☐ | 6 − 3 = ☐ | 8 − 1 = ☐ | 8 − 3 = ☐ |

Using Math

◆ How many 🐀 are left?

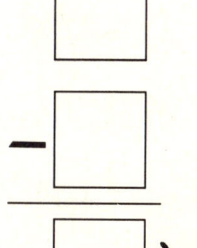

☐ − ☐ = ☐ are left.

5

Subtracting from 9

How many 🐟 are left?

| 9 | − 4 | 5 | Subtract.
9
− 4
―――
5 🐟 are left. |

Guided Practice

◆ Subtract.

9
− 3
―――
6

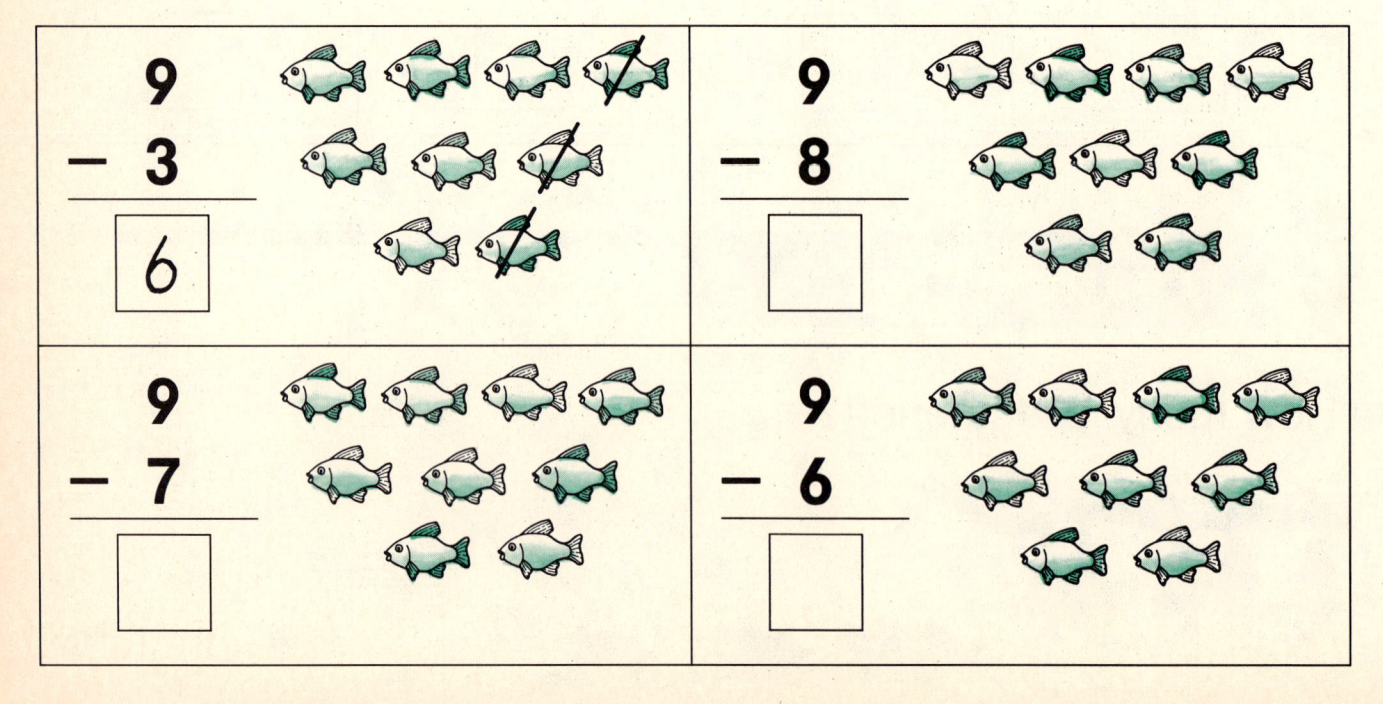

9
− 8
―――
☐

9
− 7
―――
☐

9
− 6
―――
☐

54

Practice

◆ Subtract.

9 − 2 = ☐	9 − 5 = ☐	9 − 0 = ☐

7 − 5 = ☐	9 − 3 = ☐	9 − 9 = ☐	9 − 8 = ☐

8 − 7 = ☐	9 − 1 = ☐	9 − 6 = ☐	9 − 7 = ☐

Problem Solving

◆ Write how many. Add.

☐ + ☐ = ☐ in all

55

6

Subtracting from 10

How many 🕷 are left?

| 10 | − 5 | 5 | Subtract.
10
− 5
─────
5 🕷 are left. |

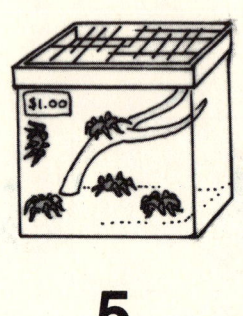

Guided Practice

◆ Subtract.

10
− 2
─────
 8

10
− 9
─────

10
− 8
─────

10
− 4
─────

56

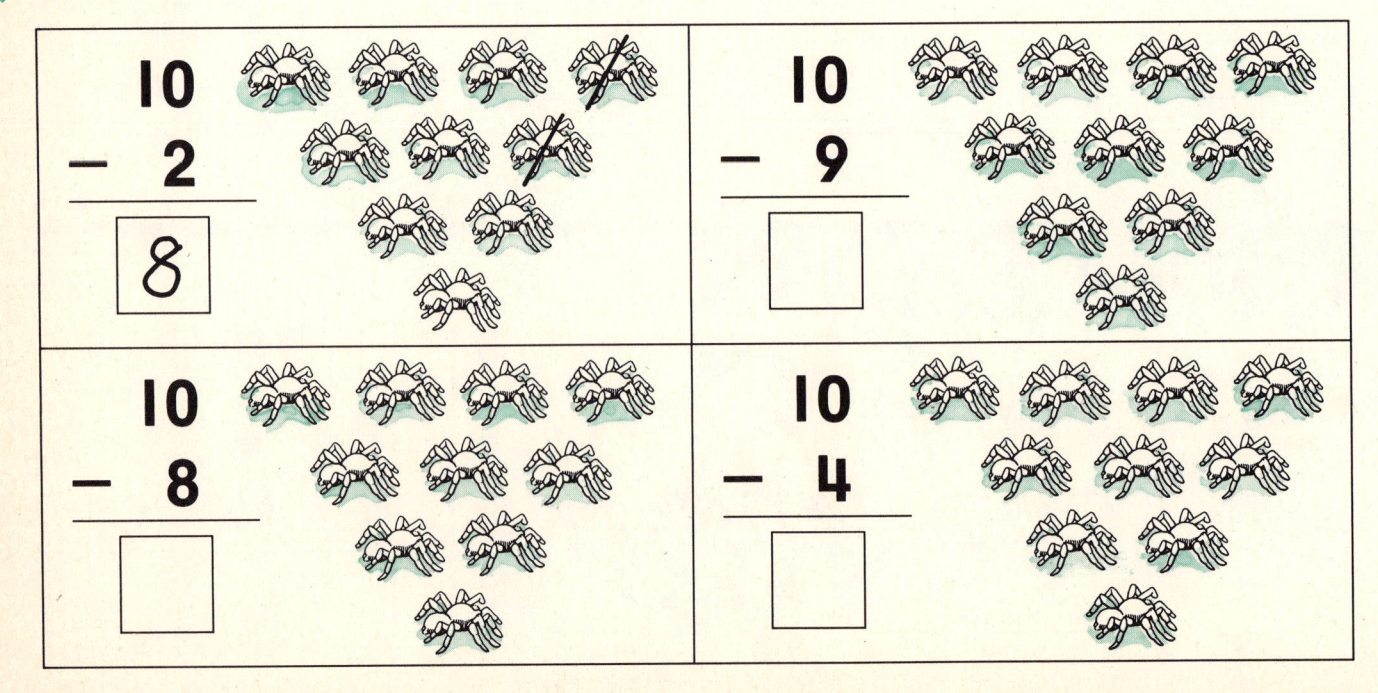

Practice

◆ Subtract.

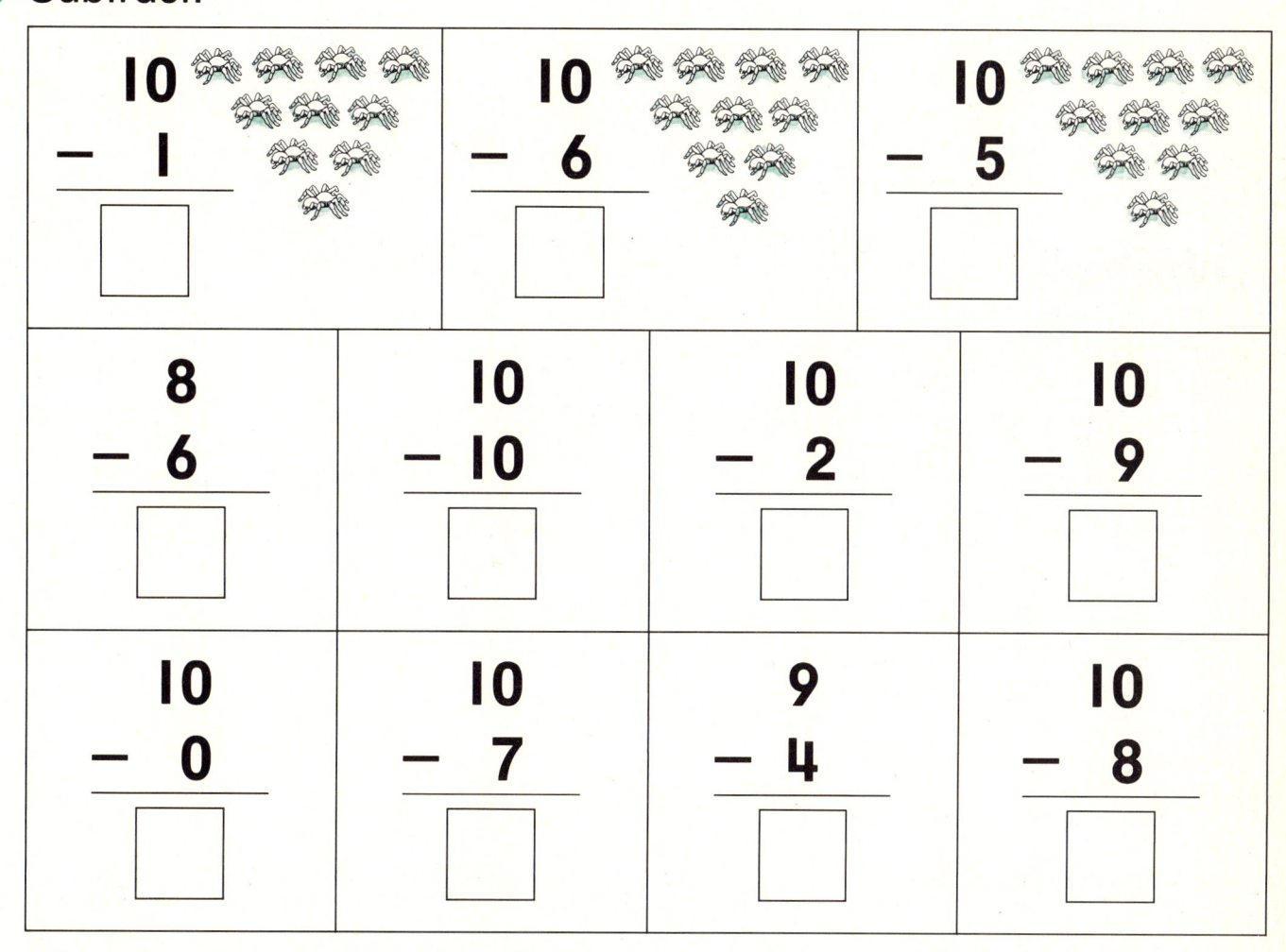

10 − 1 = ☐	10 − 6 = ☐	10 − 5 = ☐

8 − 6 = ☐	10 − 10 = ☐	10 − 2 = ☐	10 − 9 = ☐

10 − 0 = ☐	10 − 7 = ☐	9 − 4 = ☐	10 − 8 = ☐

Using Math

◆ How many are left?

☐ − ☐ = ☐ are left.

57

7

Dimes

| 1 dime
10 cents
10¢ | 1 dime
10 cents
10¢ |

Guided Practice

◆ How much money?

3¢
7¢

4¢
9¢

5¢
10¢

2¢
10¢

58

Practice

◆ Write how much money.

Using Math

◆ Ring how much money.

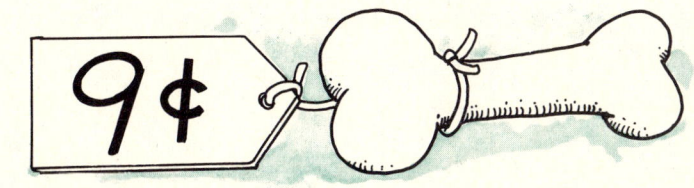

9¢

Problem Solving 8

Find a Pattern

◆ Look at the pictures.
Find the pattern.
Ring what comes next.

◆ Ring what comes next.

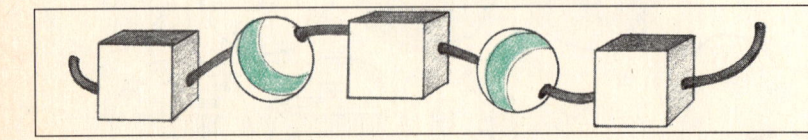

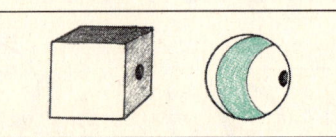

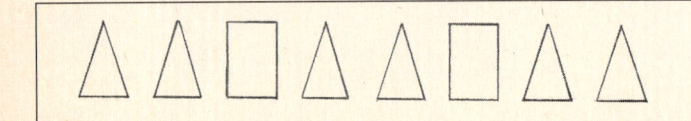

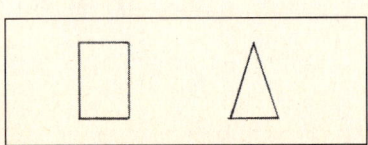

60

Practice

◆ Ring what comes next.

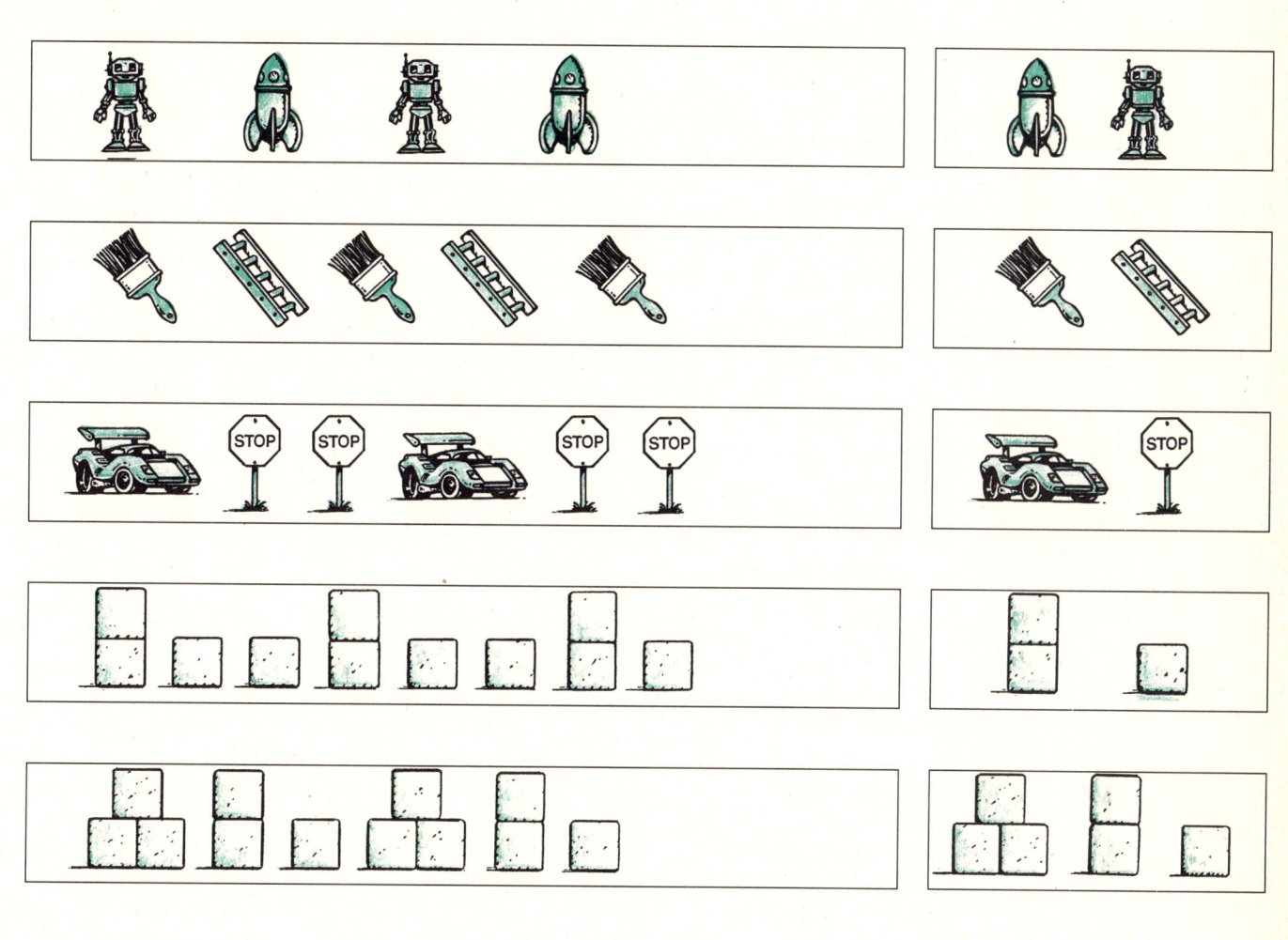

◆ Draw what comes next.

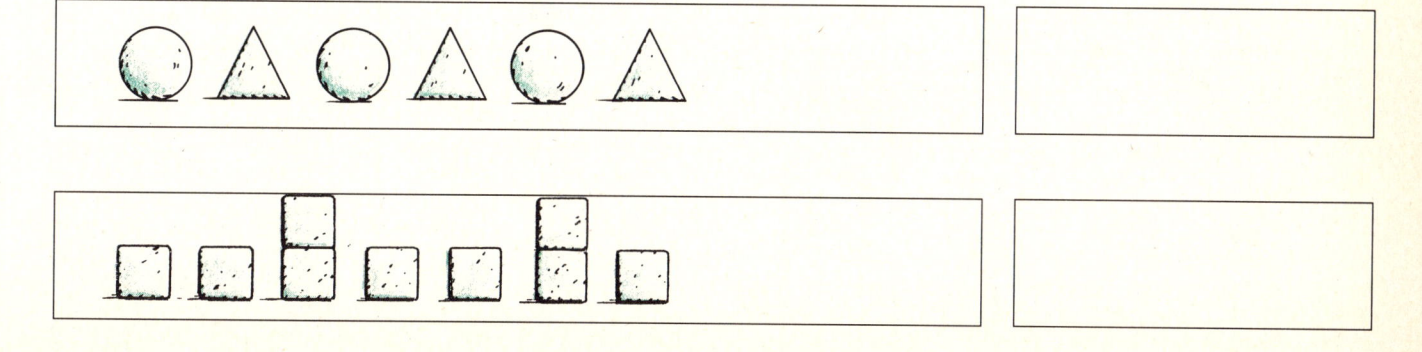

61

Review

◆ Subtract.

pages 46–47			
3 − 1	5 − 4	5 − 2	4 − 3

pages 48–49			
7 − 5	6 − 4	6 − 1	7 − 3

pages 50–51			
4 − 0	2 − 0	5 − 0	7 − 0

pages 52–53			
8 − 8	8 − 5	8 − 2	8 − 3

CHAPTER 3

◆ Subtract.

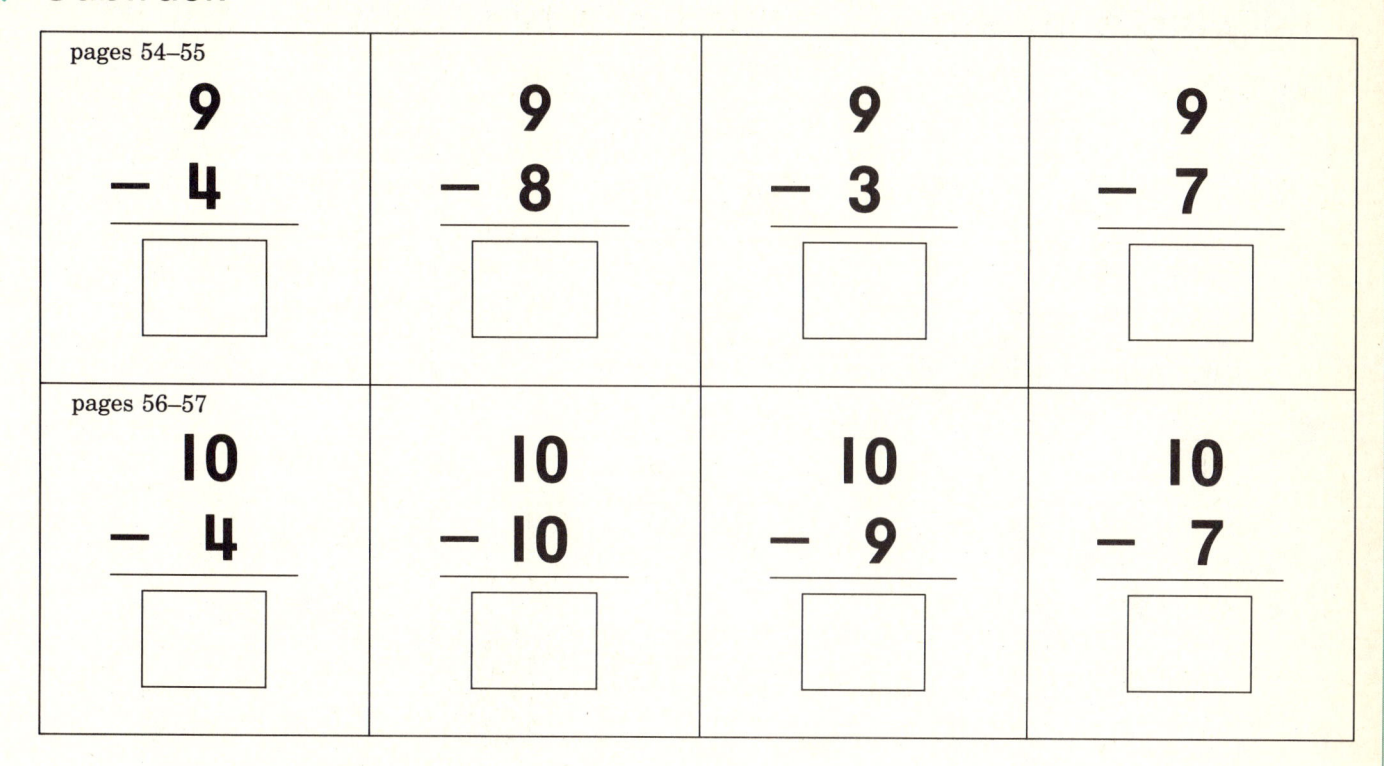

pages 54–55

9	9	9	9
− 4	− 8	− 3	− 7

pages 56–57

10	10	10	10
− 4	− 10	− 9	− 7

◆ How much money?

pages 58–59

1¢
10¢

5¢
10¢

◆ Write how much money.

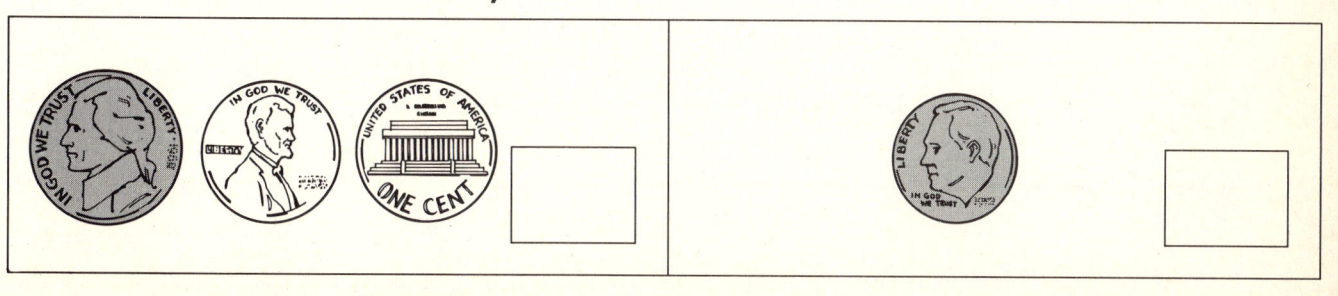

63

Review

CHAPTER 3

◆ Ring what comes next.
pages 60–61

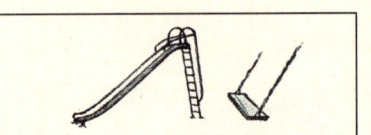

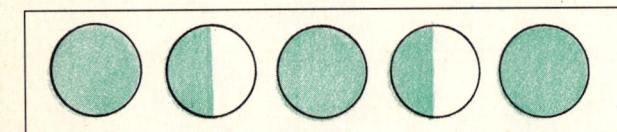

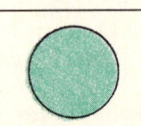

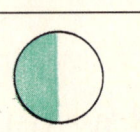

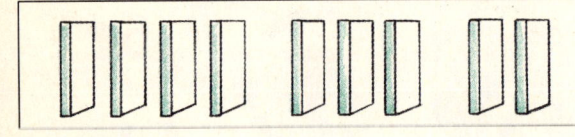

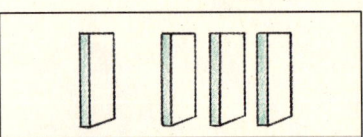

◆ Draw what comes next.

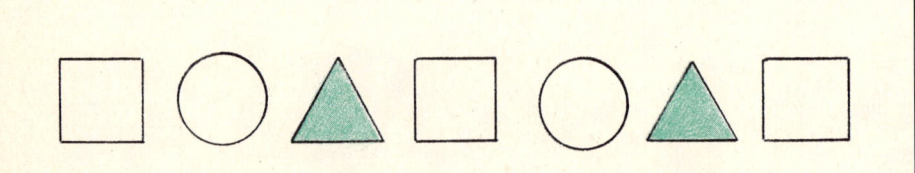

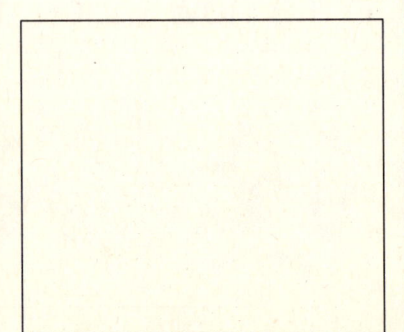

64

Test

CHAPTER 3

◆ Subtract

pages 46–49

4
− 2

5
− 3

7
− 6

6
− 2

pages 50–53

6
− 0

1
− 0

8
− 4

8
− 6

pages 54–57

9
− 1

9
− 6

10
− 5

10
− 3

◆ Write how much money.

pages 58–59

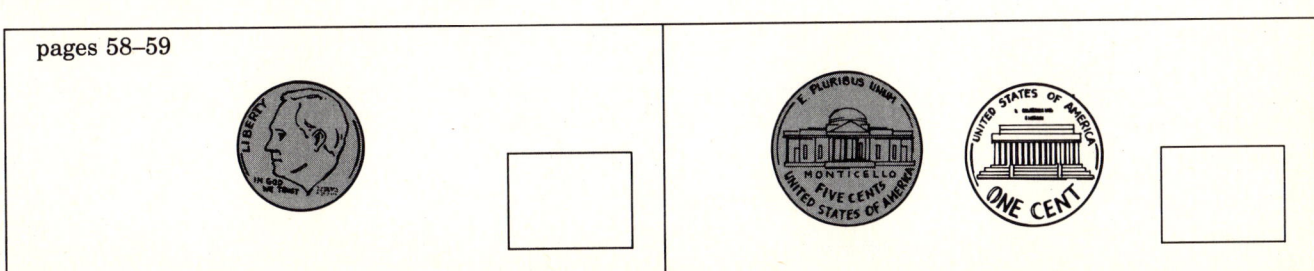

65

Test

CHAPTER 3

◆ Ring what comes next.

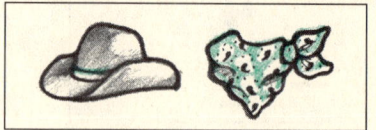

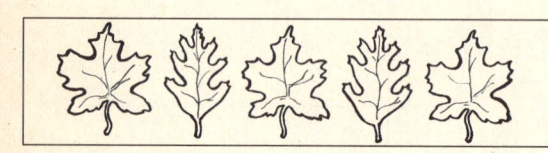

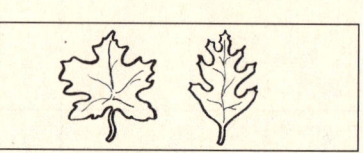

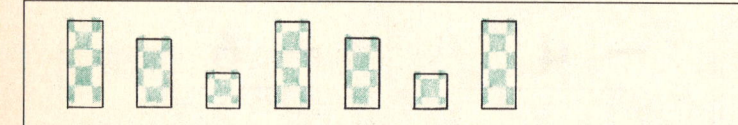

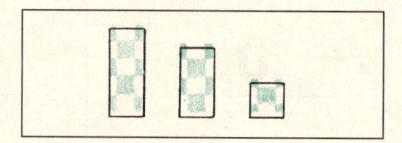

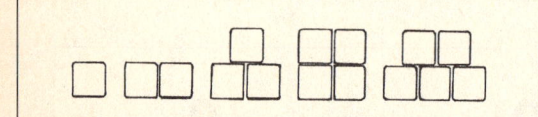

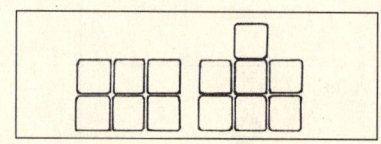

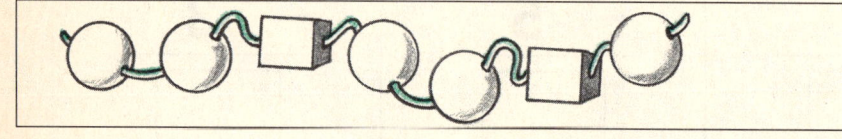

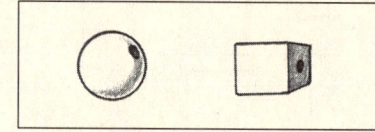

◆ Draw what comes next.

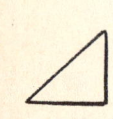

66

Cumulative Review

CHAPTER 1

◆ Write how many.

pages 2–3

pages 4–5

pages 6–7

pages 8–9

67

◆ Write how many.

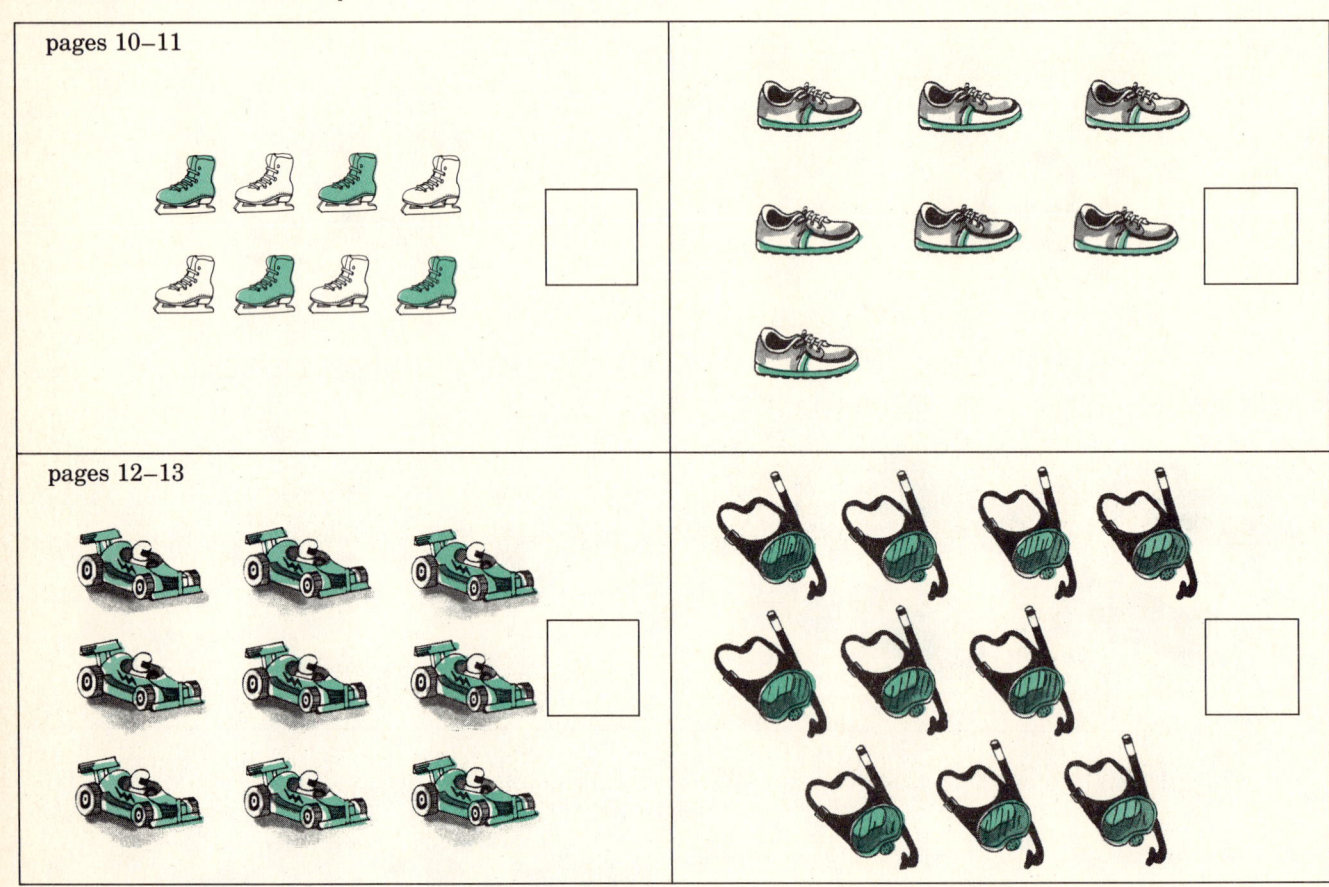

pages 10–11

pages 12–13

◆ Write how much money.
pages 14–15

68

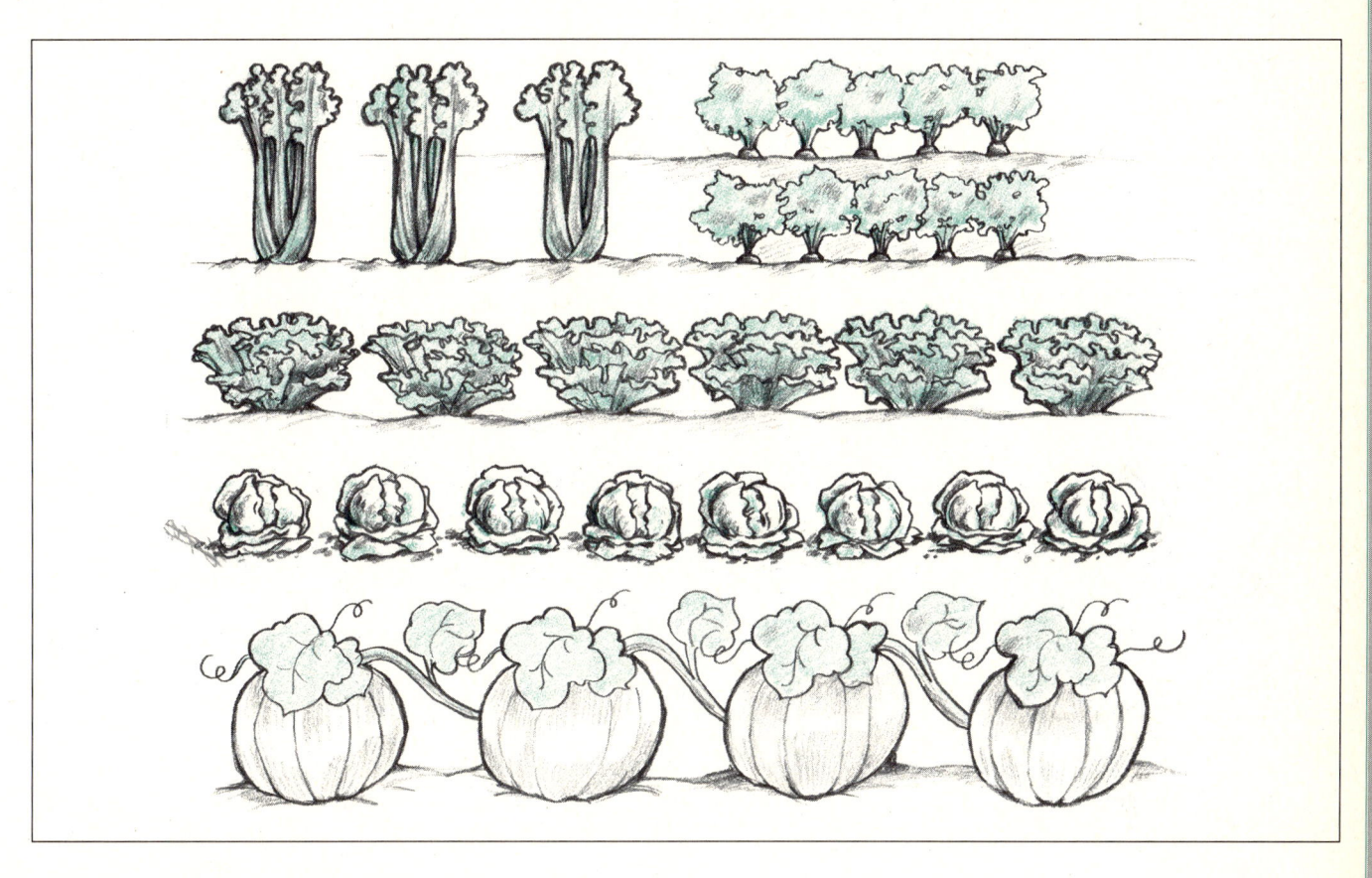

♦ Count the pictures.

Write how many.

pages 16–17

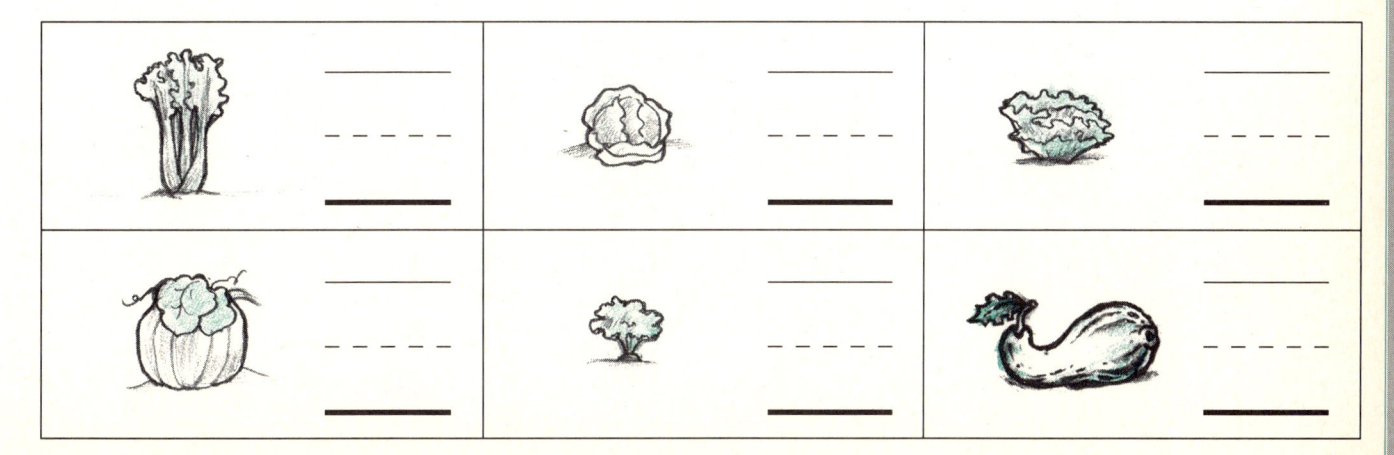

CHAPTER 2

◆ Add.

pages 24–25			
1 + 1 = ☐	1 + 2 = ☐	3 + 2 = ☐	3 + 1 = ☐

pages 26–27			
3 + 3 = ☐	1 + 5 = ☐	2 + 5 = ☐	3 + 4 = ☐

pages 28–29			
4 + 0 = ☐	0 + 6 = ☐	0 + 5 = ☐	1 + 0 = ☐

pages 30–31			
4 + 4 = ☐	4 + 3 = ☐	5 + 3 = ☐	6 + 2 = ☐

◆ Add.

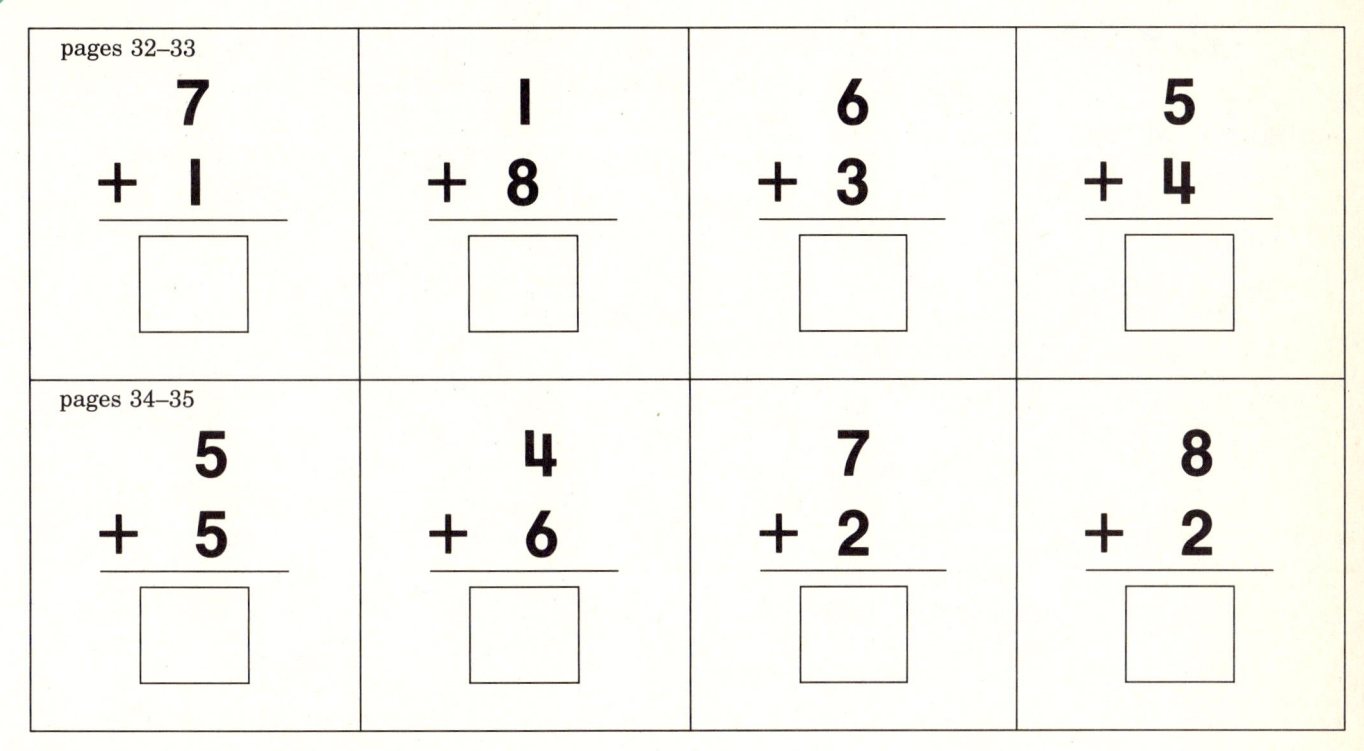

pages 32–33

$\begin{array}{r}7\\+\ 1\\\hline\end{array}$

$\begin{array}{r}1\\+\ 8\\\hline\end{array}$

$\begin{array}{r}6\\+\ 3\\\hline\end{array}$

$\begin{array}{r}5\\+\ 4\\\hline\end{array}$

pages 34–35

$\begin{array}{r}5\\+\ 5\\\hline\end{array}$

$\begin{array}{r}4\\+\ 6\\\hline\end{array}$

$\begin{array}{r}7\\+\ 2\\\hline\end{array}$

$\begin{array}{r}8\\+\ 2\\\hline\end{array}$

◆ Write how much money.

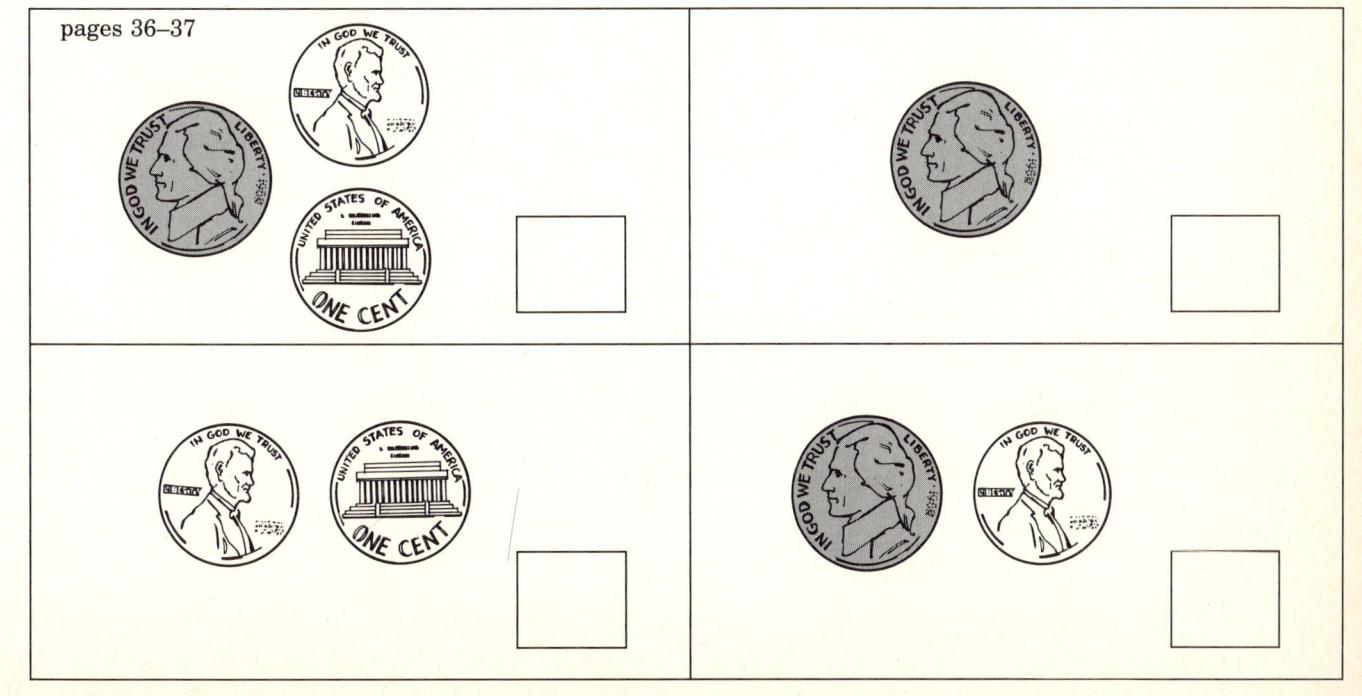

pages 36–37

71

◆ Look at the picture.

Write how many. Add.

pages 38–39

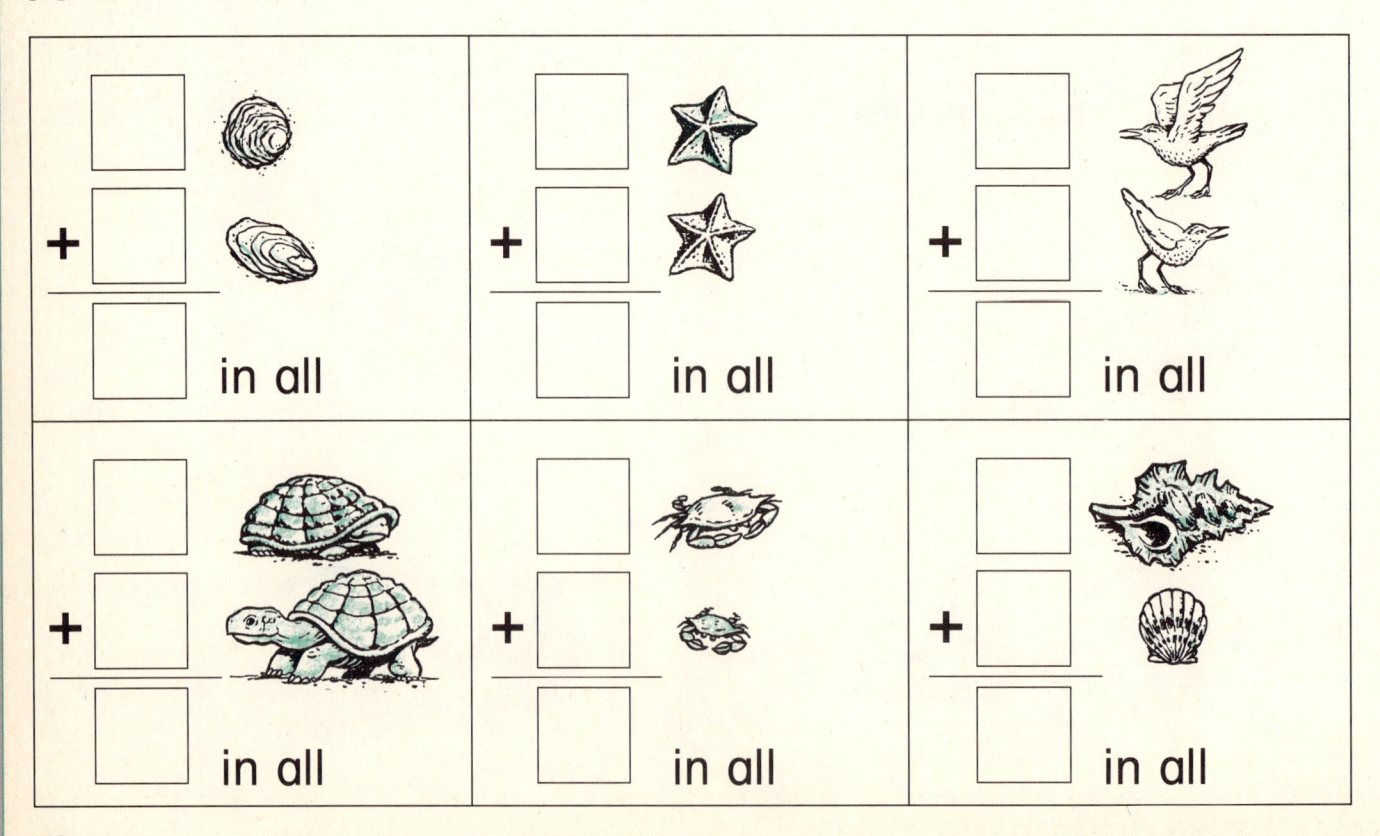

in all

in all

in all

in all

in all

in all

72

CHAPTER 3

◆ Subtract.

pages 46–49

4	5	7	6
− 2	− 1	− 3	− 4

pages 50–53

5	7	8	8
− 0	− 0	− 7	− 3

pages 54–57

9	9	10	10
− 6	− 5	− 2	− 7

◆ Write how much money.

pages 58–59

73

◆ Ring what comes next.
pages 60–61

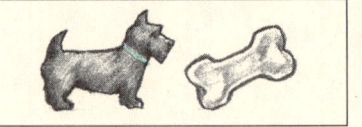

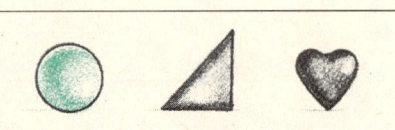

◆ Draw what comes next.

74

Name _____

CHAPTER 4

Place Value Through 99

About 90 racers rode in the race.
About how many racers are in the picture?
Are all of the racers in the picture?
How do you know?

1

Tens and Ones to 19

Group 10 **ones** to make 1 **ten**.

10 ones = 1 ten

12 = 1 ten 2 ones

Guided Practice

◆ How many?

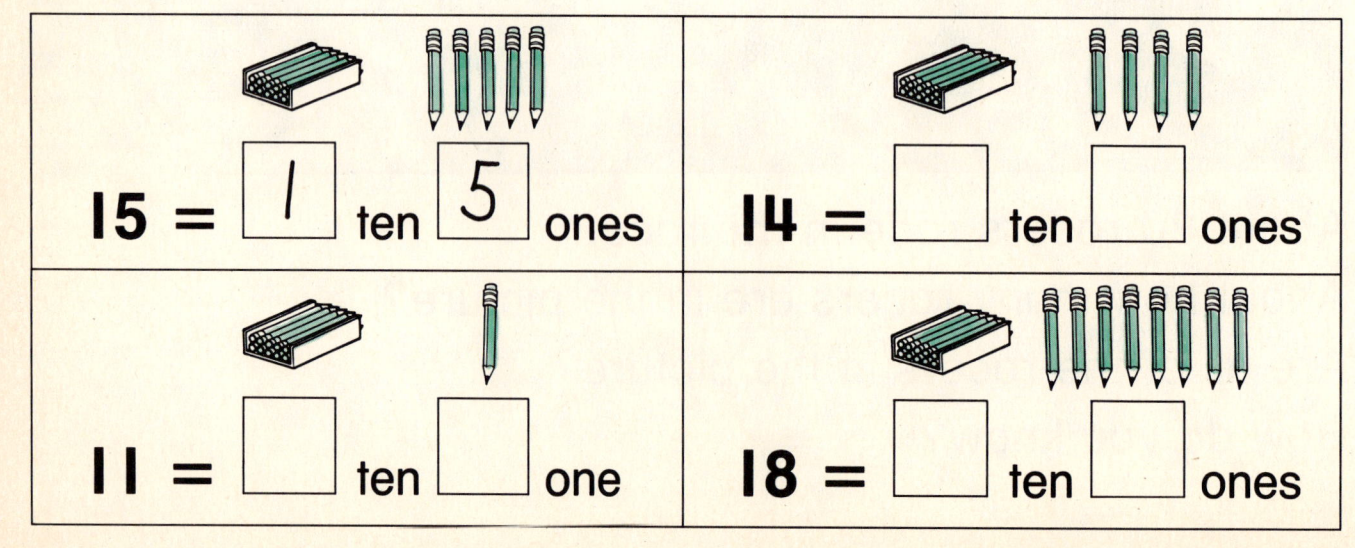

15 = ☐1☐ ten ☐5☐ ones

14 = ☐ ten ☐ ones

11 = ☐ ten ☐ one

18 = ☐ ten ☐ ones

76

Practice

◆ How many?

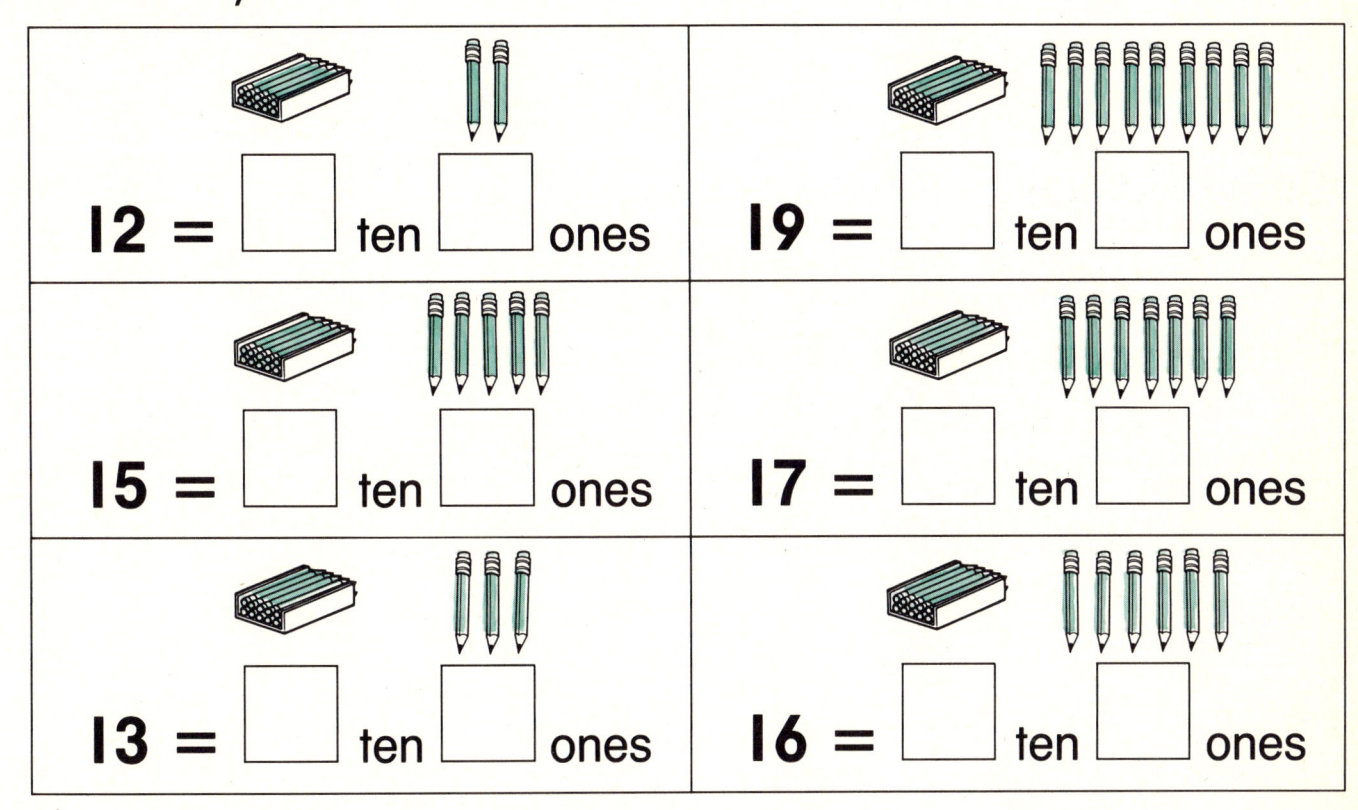

12 = ☐ ten ☐ ones

19 = ☐ ten ☐ ones

15 = ☐ ten ☐ ones

17 = ☐ ten ☐ ones

13 = ☐ ten ☐ ones

16 = ☐ ten ☐ ones

Using Math

◆ Ring 10.

How many tens? ☐

How many ones? ☐

How many in all? ☐

2

Tens and Ones to 39

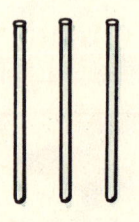

23 = 2 tens   3 ones

Guided Practice

◆ How many?

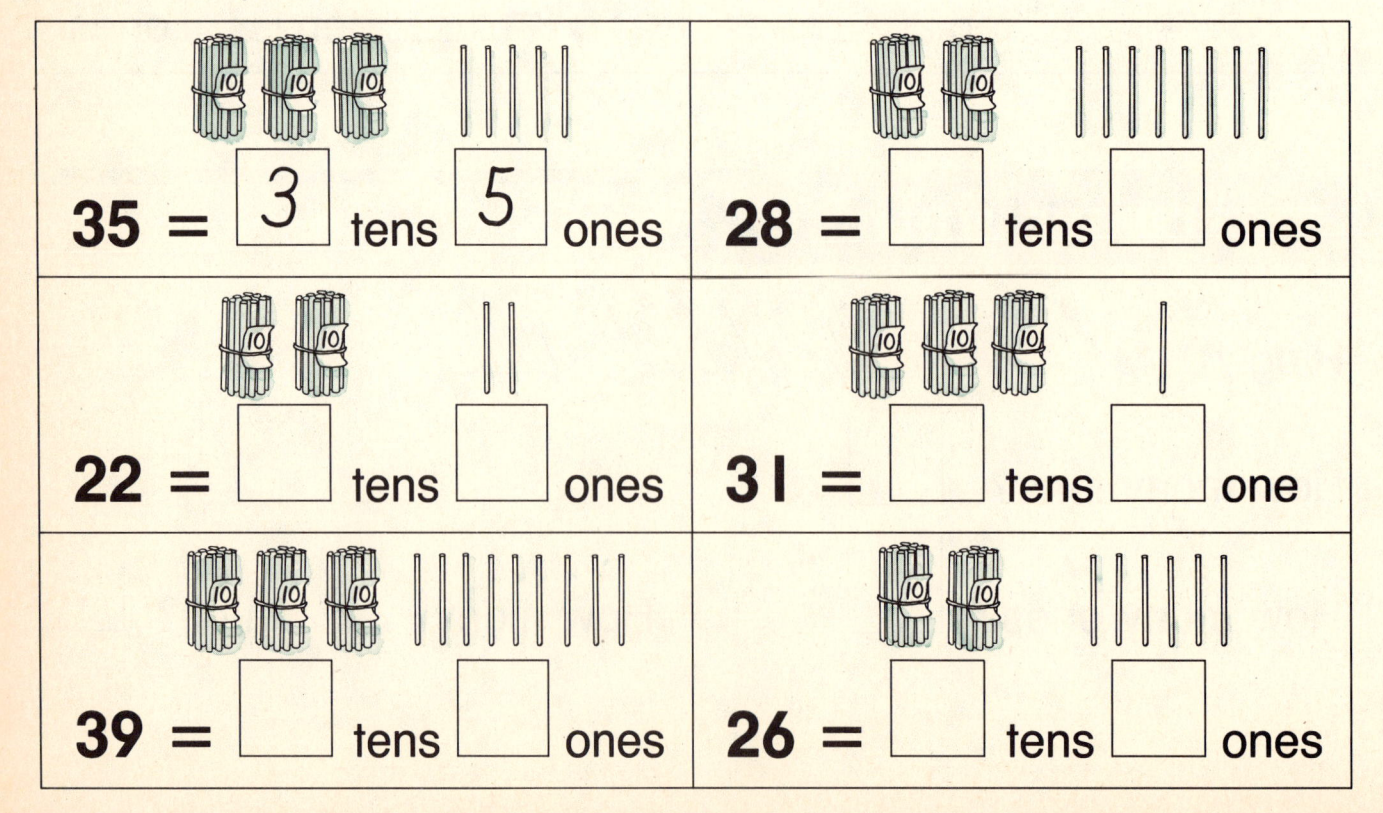

35 = [3] tens [5] ones

28 = [ ] tens [ ] ones

22 = [ ] tens [ ] ones

31 = [ ] tens [ ] one

39 = [ ] tens [ ] ones

26 = [ ] tens [ ] ones

Practice

◆ How many?

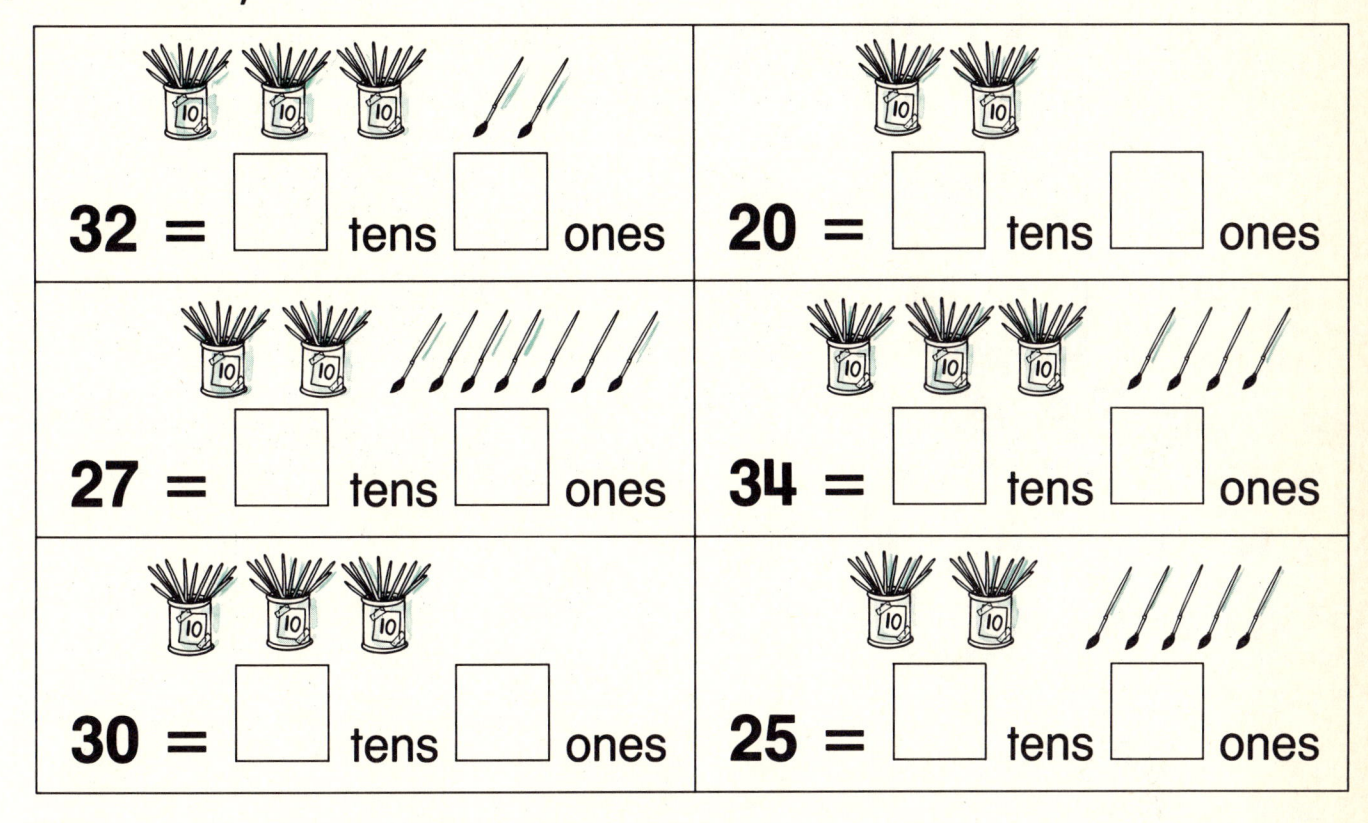

32 = ☐ tens ☐ ones

20 = ☐ tens ☐ ones

27 = ☐ tens ☐ ones

34 = ☐ tens ☐ ones

30 = ☐ tens ☐ ones

25 = ☐ tens ☐ ones

Using Math

◆ Ring groups of 10.

How many tens? ☐

How many ones? ☐

How many in all? ☐

3

Tens and Ones to 59

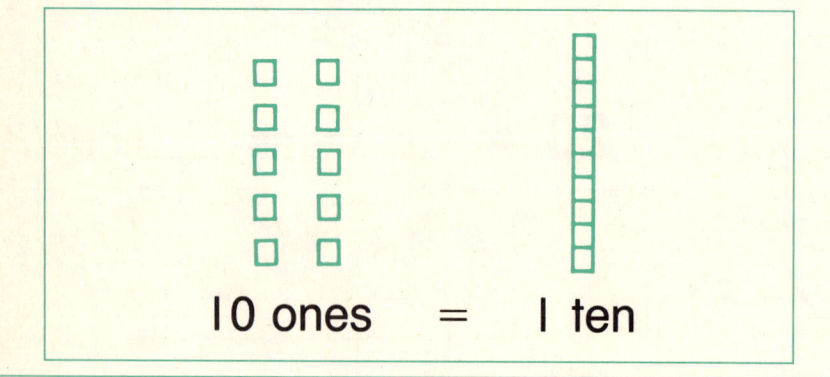

10 ones = 1 ten

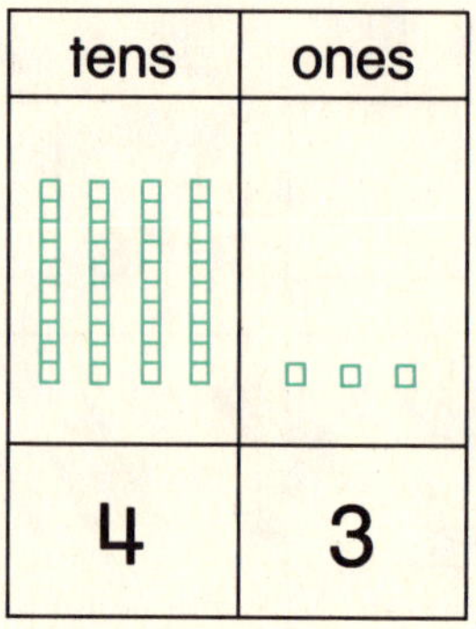

tens	ones
4	3	= 43

Guided Practice

◆ How many?

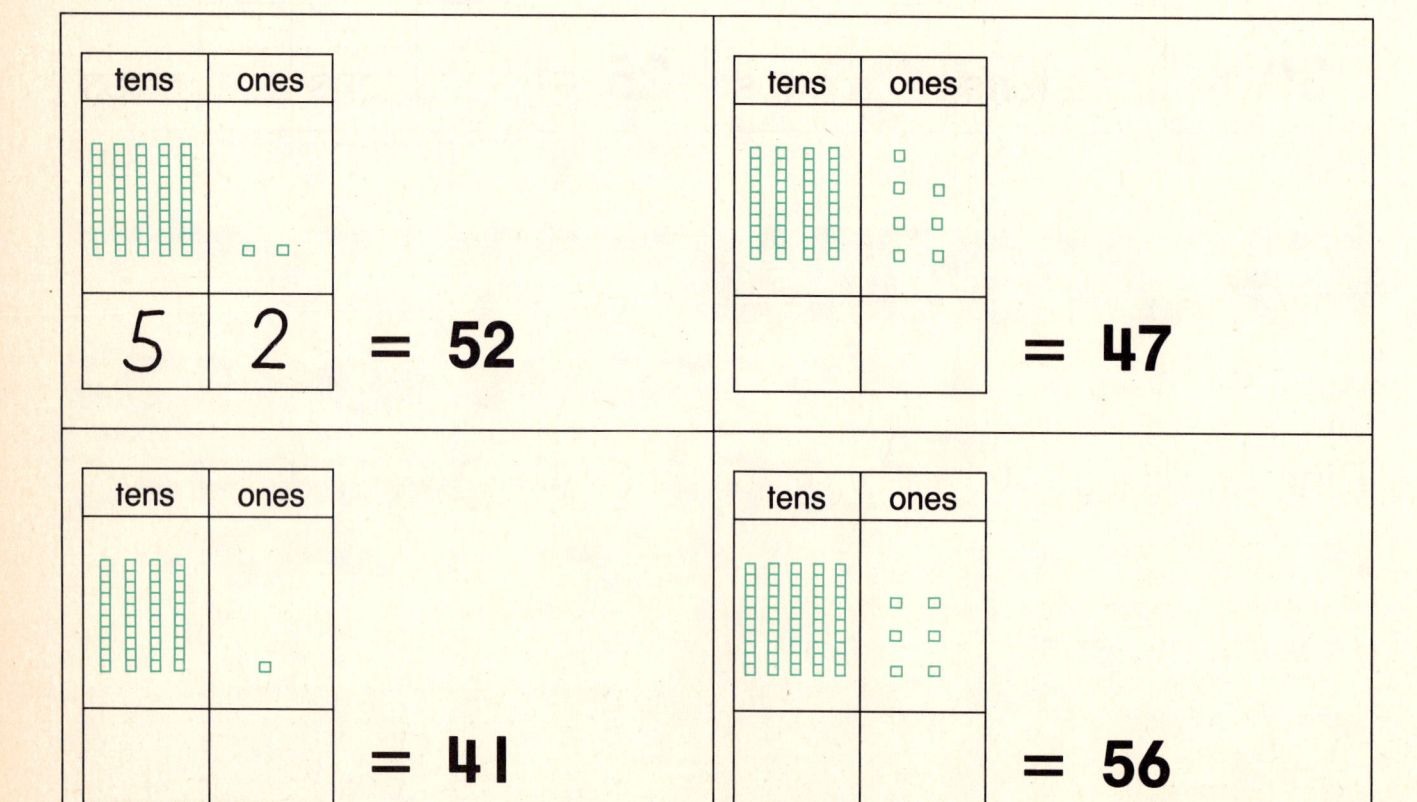

tens	ones
5	2	= 52

tens	ones
		= 47

tens	ones
		= 41

tens	ones
		= 56

80

Practice

◆ How many?

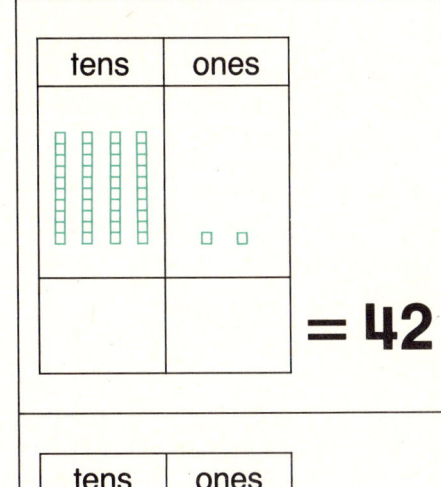

tens	ones	
(4 tens)	(2 ones)	= 42
(5 tens)	(4 ones)	= 54
(5 tens)	(0 ones)	= 50
(4 tens)	(8 ones)	= 48
(4 tens)	(5 ones)	= 45
(5 tens)	(9 ones)	= 59

Using Math

◆ Mary has 51 📓.
Circle how many groups of 10 📓 Mary has.

1   2   3   4   5   6

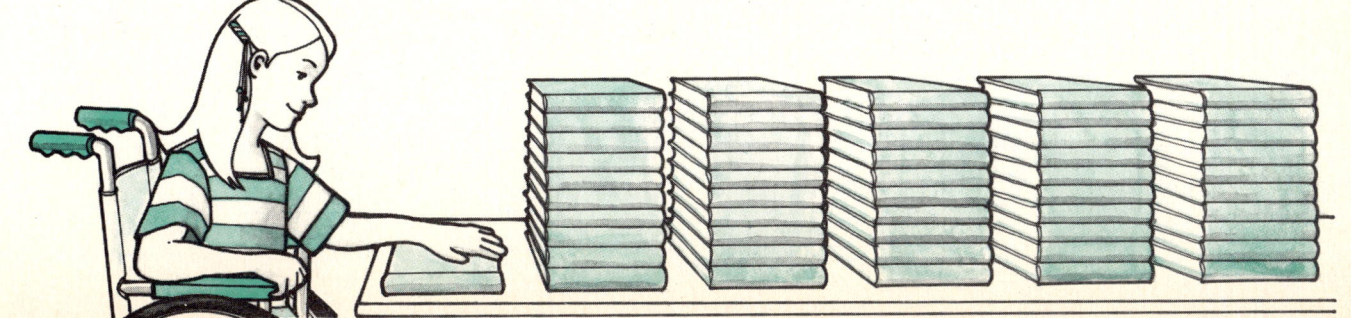

81

4

Tens and Ones to 79

tens	ones
6	8

= 68

Guided Practice

◆ How many?

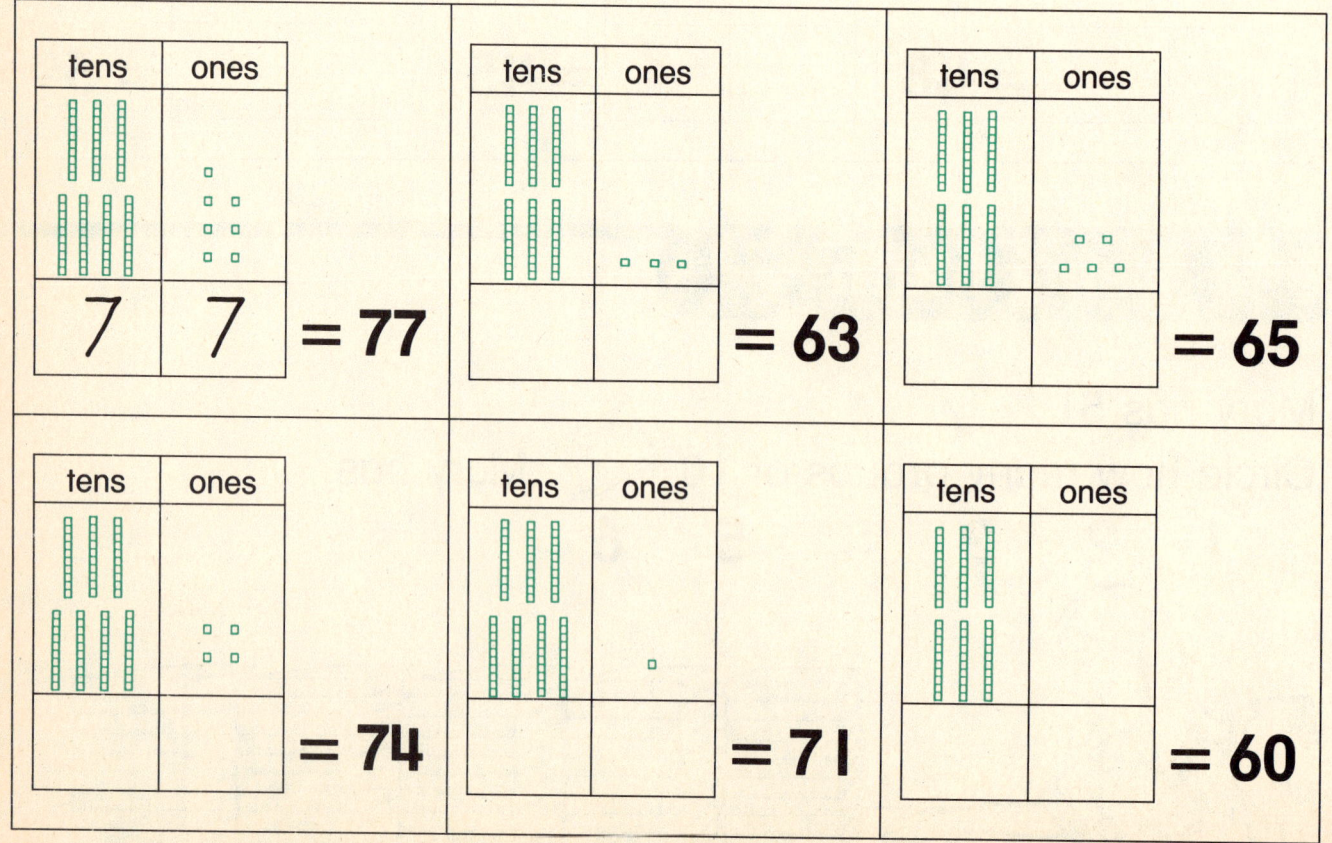

tens	ones
7	7

= 77

= 63

= 65

= 74

= 71

= 60

82

Practice

◆ How many?

tens	ones		tens	ones		tens	ones
= 75			= 67			= 69	

tens	ones		tens	ones		tens	ones
= 70			= 72			= 66	

Using Math

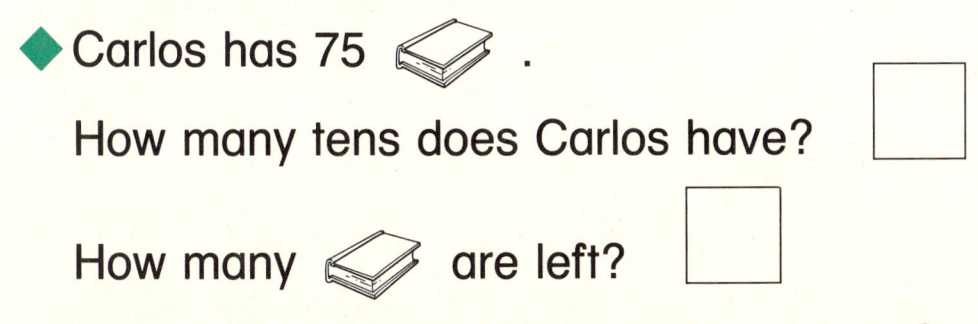

◆ Carlos has 75 books.

How many tens does Carlos have? ☐

How many books are left? ☐

5

Tens and Ones to 99

tens	ones
||||	∷∷
8	7	= 87

Guided Practice

◆ How many?

tens	ones	
||	∷	
9	2	= 92

tens	ones	
||||	∷	
		= ☐

tens	ones	
|||	∷∷	
		= ☐

tens	ones	
||||	∷	
		= ☐

tens	ones	
||||	∷∷	
		= ☐

tens	ones	
||||		
		= ☐

84

Practice

◆ How many?

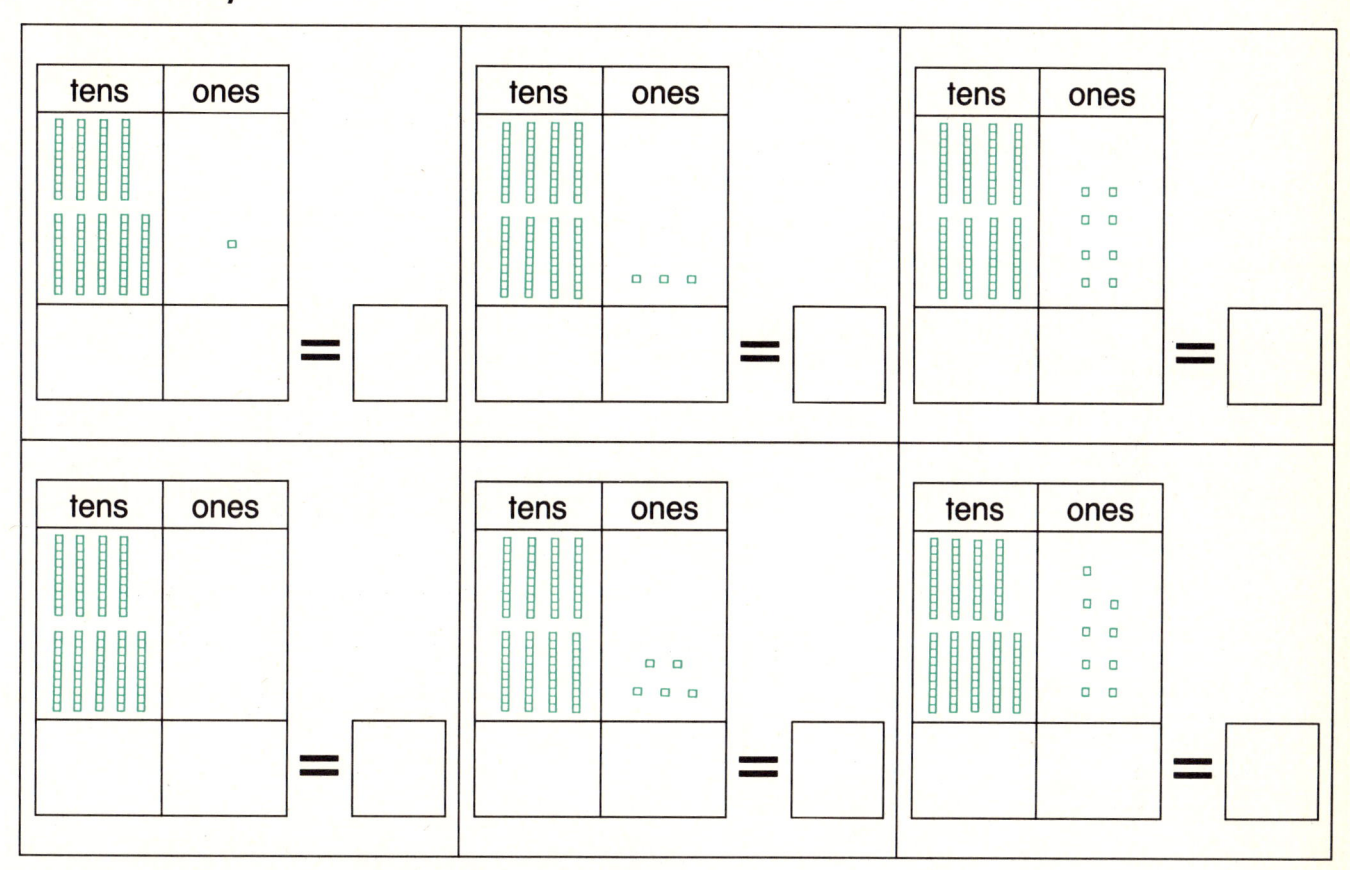

Problem Solving

◆ Draw what comes next.

85

6

Ordering Numbers to 99

You count numbers in order.

Guided Practice

◆ Write each missing number.

21	22	23	24	25	26		28	29	30
31		33	34		36	37	38		40
	42	43		45			48	49	50
51			54		56	57	58	59	
	62	63	64	65				69	70
71	72			75	76	77	78		80

86

Practice

◆ Write each missing number.

13	14		16

17	18		20

32		34	35

	37	38	

53	54		

57		59	

81	82		84

85	86		88

92			95

96		98	

Using Math

◆ Start with 60.
Connect the dots in order.

7

Quarters

| 1 quarter
25 cents
25¢  | 1 quarter
25 cents
25¢  |

Guided Practice

◆ How much money?

12¢
27¢

5¢
25¢

5¢
25¢

12¢
27¢

88

Practice

◆ Write how much money.

quarter ☐	dime ☐
quarter + penny ☐	dime + penny ☐
quarter + penny + penny + penny ☐	dime + penny + penny ☐

Using Math

◆ Ring how much money.

GLUE 13¢   quarter dime penny penny penny

89

Problem Solving 8

Find a Pattern

These numbers make a pattern.

2 4 6 8 10 12

Guided Practice

◆ Write the numbers to complete a pattern.

| 11 | 12 | 13 | 14 | 15 | 16 | 17 | 18 | 19 | 20 |

| 8 | 10 | 12 | 14 | | | 22 | 24 |

| 1 | 3 | 5 | | | 11 | 13 | | 17 | 19 |

| 10 | 20 | | 40 | | 70 | | 90 |

90

Practice

◆ Write the numbers to complete a pattern.

| 26 | 28 | 30 | | | | 38 | | 42 | |

| 21 | 23 | | 27 | | | 33 | 35 | | |

| 70 | 71 | 72 | | | 75 | | | 78 | |

| 15 | 20 | 25 | | | 45 | | | | |

| 10 | | 30 | 40 | | | | 80 | | |

| 82 | 83 | 84 | 85 | | | | | | |

◆ Use numbers to make a pattern of your own.

Review

◆ How many?

pages 76–77

15 = ☐ ten ☐ ones

18 = ☐ ten ☐ ones

pages 78–79

23 = ☐ tens ☐ ones

34 = ☐ tens ☐ ones

pages 80–81

tens	ones

=

tens	ones

=

pages 82–83

tens	ones

=

tens	ones

=

92

CHAPTER 4

◆ How many?

pages 84–85

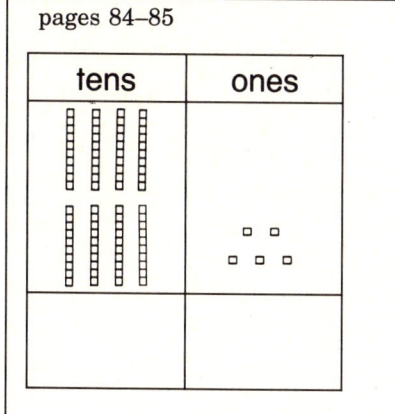

tens	ones
‖‖‖‖	⸭

☐ = ☐

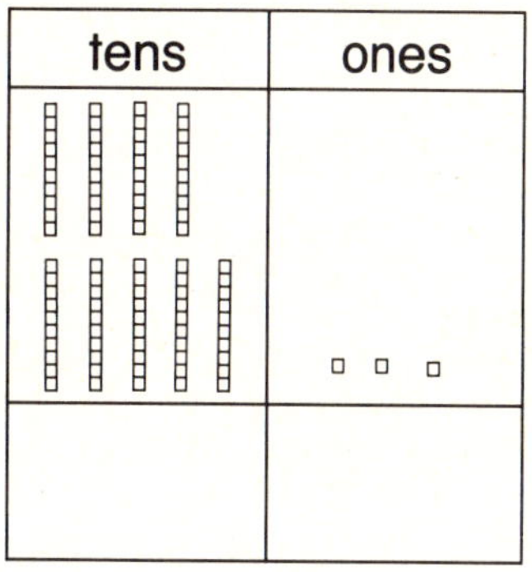

tens	ones
‖‖‖‖‖	▫ ▫ ▫

☐ = ☐

◆ Write each missing number.

pages 86–87

31	32		34

80			83

◆ How much money?

pages 88–89

3¢
12¢

16¢
26¢

◆ Write how much money.

☐

☐

93

Review

CHAPTER 4

◆ **Write the numbers to complete a pattern.**
pages 90–91

| 38 | 40 | 42 | | | | 50 | | 54 | |

| 51 | 53 | | 57 | | | 63 | 65 | | |

| 8 | 9 | 10 | | | 13 | | | 16 | |

| 5 | 10 | 15 | | | | 35 | | | |

| | 20 | 30 | | | 50 | | | 90 | |

| 64 | 65 | 66 | 67 | | | | | | |

◆ **Use numbers to make a pattern of your own.**

| | | | | | | | | | |

94

Test

CHAPTER 4

◆ How many?

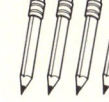

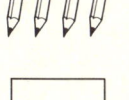

= ☐ ten ☐ ones

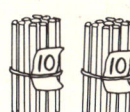

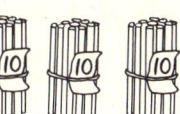

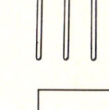

= ☐ tens ☐ ones

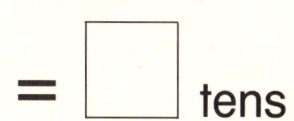

tens 	ones 

= ☐

tens 	ones 

= ☐

◆ Write each missing number.

| 15 | | 17 | |

| 61 | | | 64 |

◆ Write how much money.

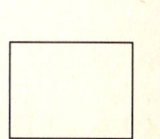

95

Test

CHAPTER 4

◆ Write the numbers to complete a pattern.

| 2 | 4 | 6 | | | | 14 | | 18 | |

| 13 | 15 | | 19 | | | 25 | 27 | | |

| 76 | 77 | 78 | | | 81 | | | 84 | |

| 15 | 20 | 25 | | | | | | 55 | |

| 10 | | 30 | | 50 | | 70 | | | |

| 90 | 91 | 92 | 93 | | | | | | |

◆ Use numbers to make a pattern of your own.

| | | | | | | | | | |

96

Name _____

CHAPTER 5

Addition and Subtraction Facts Through 12

How many students are planting new trees?
How many new trees are the students planting?
Are there more students or more new trees?
How do you know?

97

1

Adding to 11

How many 🏐 in all?

Add.

 6
+5
---
 11   🏐 in all.

Guided Practice

◆ Add.

   9
+ 2

 11

   8
+ 3

 ☐

   6
+ 5

 ☐

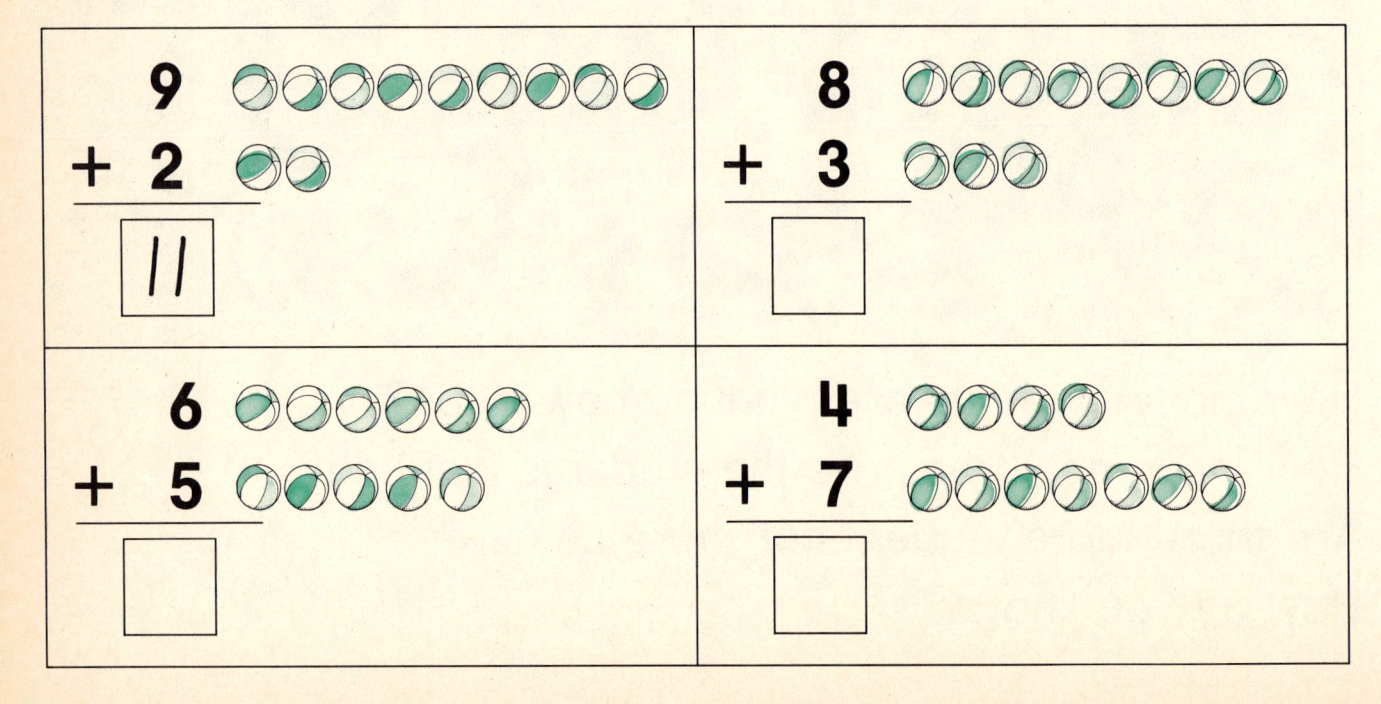

   4
+ 7

 ☐

Practice

◆ Add.

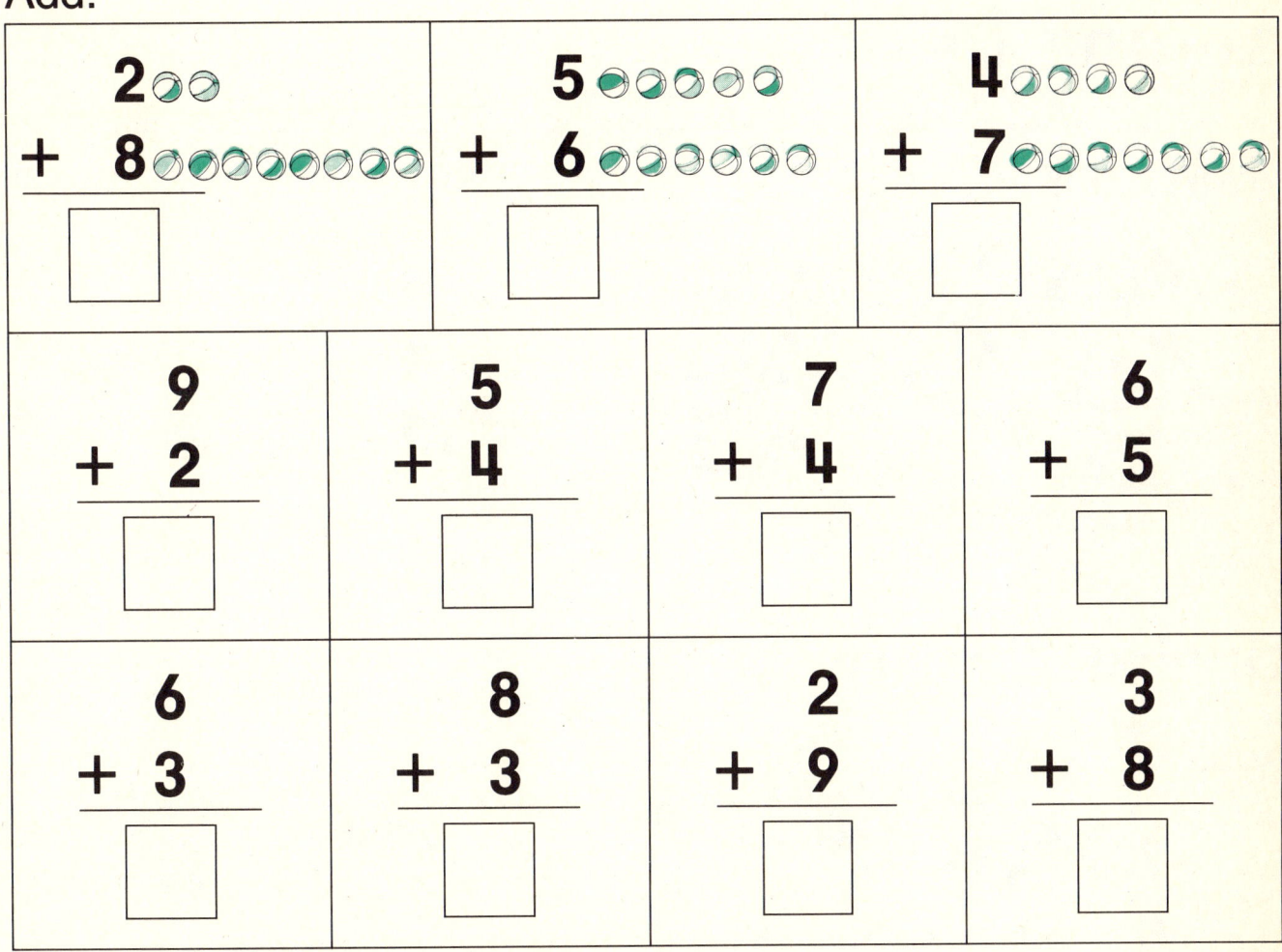

| 2 ○○
+ 8 ○○○○○○○○
☐ | 5 ○○○○○
+ 6 ○○○○○○
☐ | 4 ○○○○
+ 7 ○○○○○○○
☐ |

| 9
+ 2
───
☐ | 5
+ 4
───
☐ | 7
+ 4
───
☐ | 6
+ 5
───
☐ |
| 6
+ 3
───
☐ | 8
+ 3
───
☐ | 2
+ 9
───
☐ | 3
+ 8
───
☐ |

Using Math

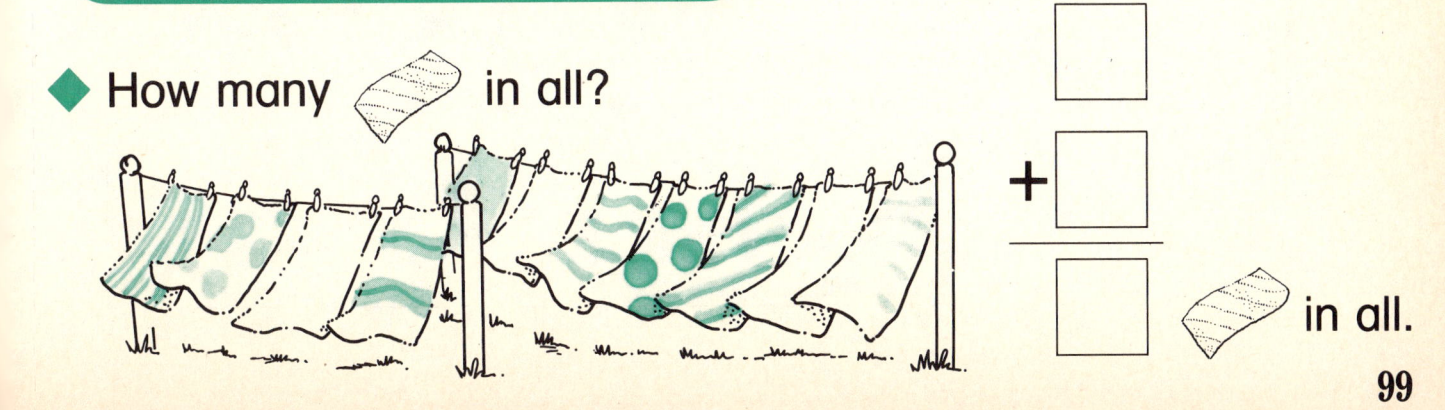

◆ How many 🧻 in all?

☐
+ ☐
───
☐ in all.

2

Adding to 12

How many 🏕 in all?

Add.

$$\begin{array}{r}8\\+4\\\hline 12\end{array}$$ 🏕 in all.

Guided Practice

◆ Add.

$$\begin{array}{r}7\\+5\\\hline 12\end{array}$$

$$\begin{array}{r}9\\+3\\\hline\end{array}$$

$$\begin{array}{r}4\\+8\\\hline\end{array}$$

$$\begin{array}{r}5\\+7\\\hline\end{array}$$

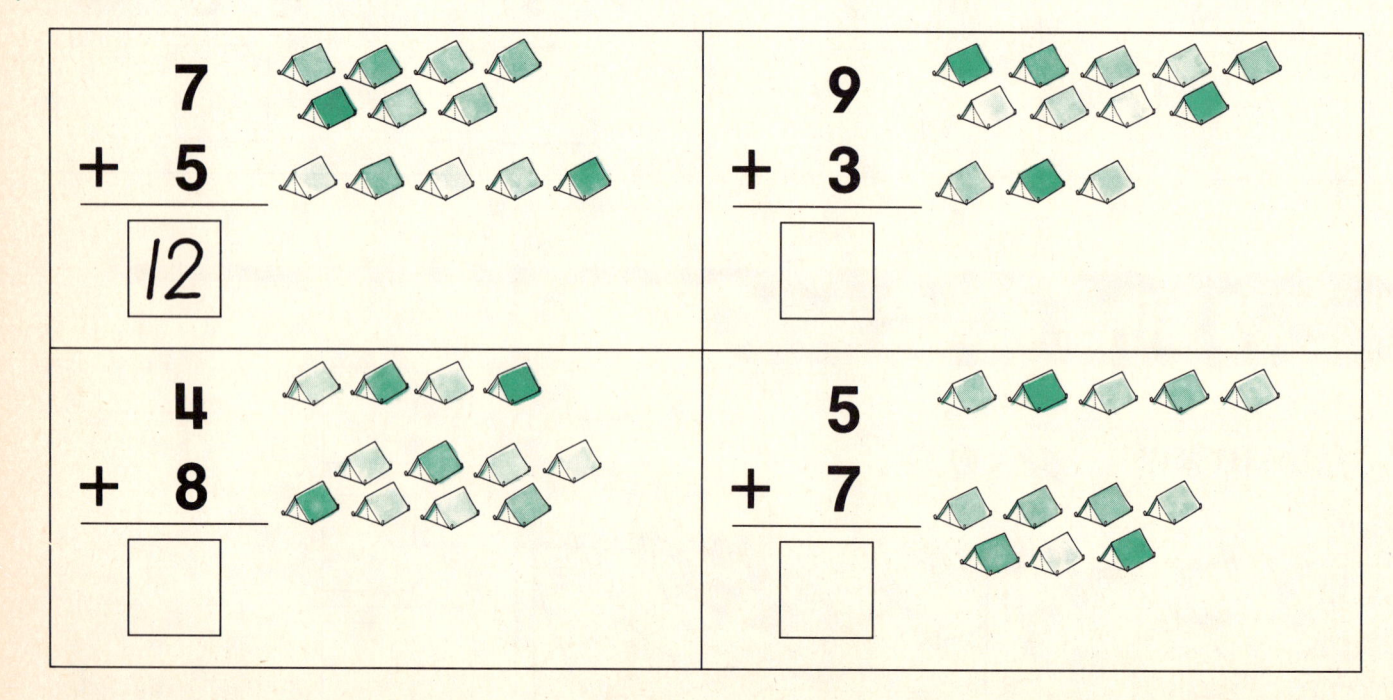

100

Practice

◆ Add.

8 + 4 ☐	6 + 5 ☐	6 + 6 ☐

3 + 9 ☐	8 + 2 ☐	4 + 8 ☐	5 + 7 ☐
7 + 5 ☐	7 + 3 ☐	9 + 3 ☐	8 + 3 ☐

Using Math

◆ How many 🐿 in all?

☐
+ ☐
———
☐ in all.

3

Subtracting from 11

How many  are left?

| 11 | − 6 | 5 | Subtract.
11
− 6
—
5   are left. |

Guided Practice

◆ Subtract.

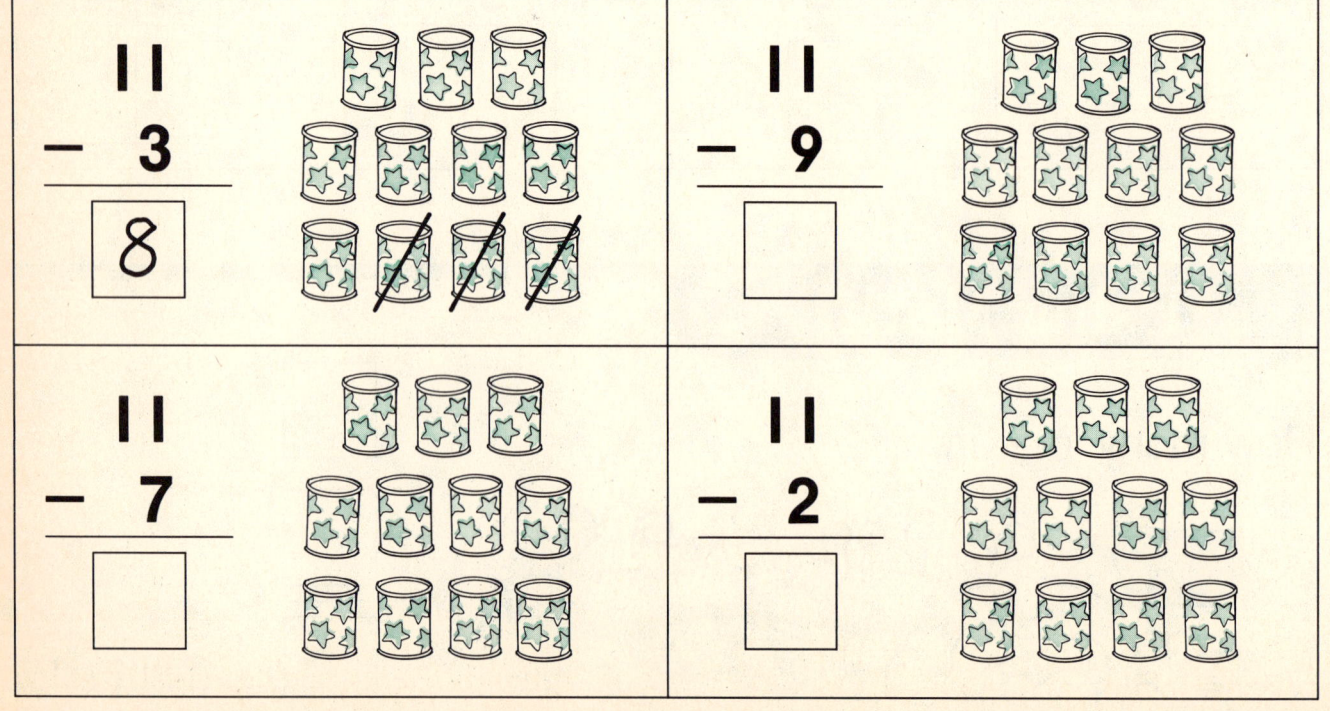

11
− 3
―
8

11
− 9
―
☐

11
− 7
―
☐

11
− 2
―
☐

102

Practice

◆ Subtract.

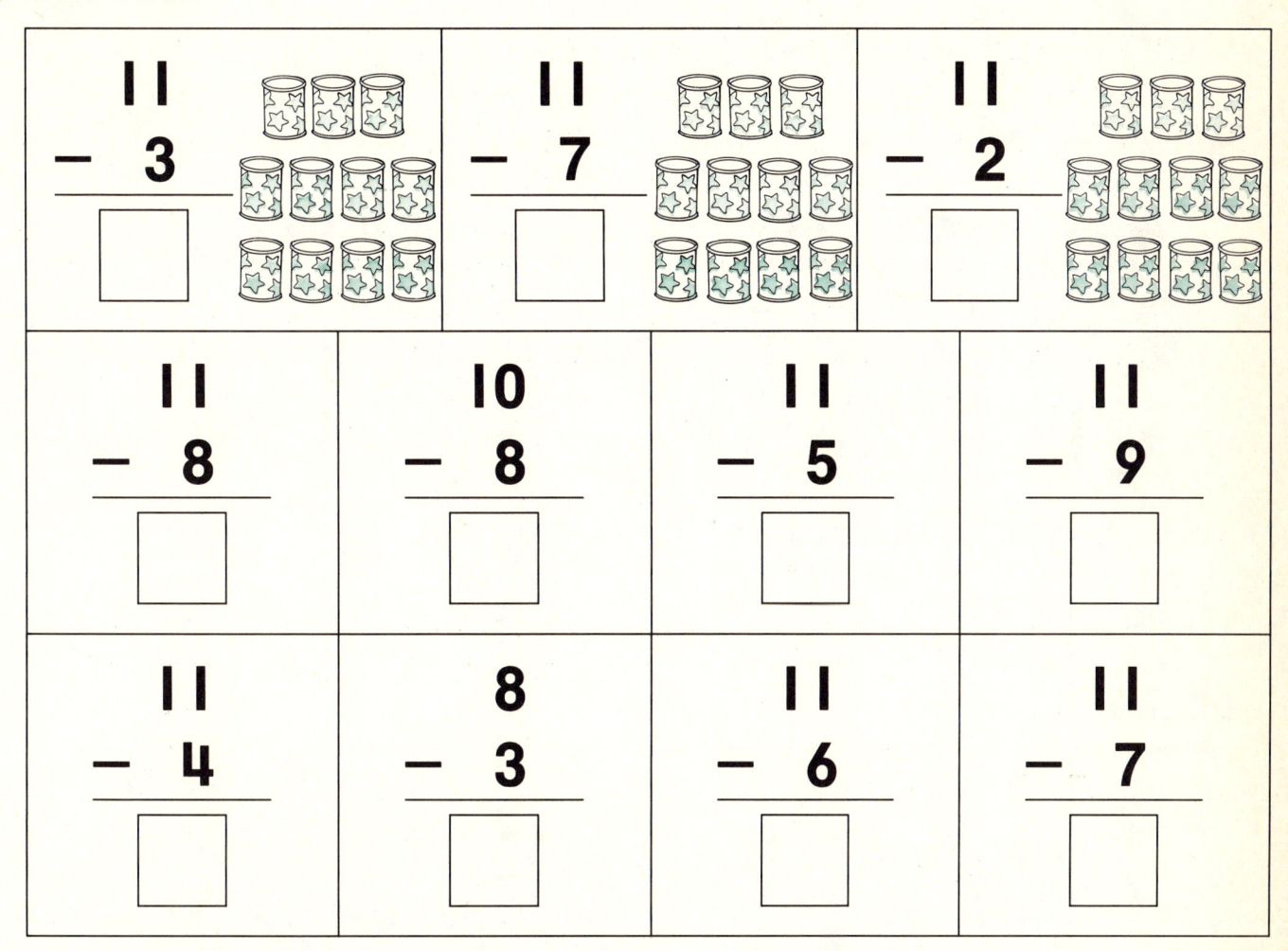

11 − 3 = ☐	11 − 7 = ☐	11 − 2 = ☐

11 − 8 = ☐	10 − 8 = ☐	11 − 5 = ☐	11 − 9 = ☐

11 − 4 = ☐	8 − 3 = ☐	11 − 6 = ☐	11 − 7 = ☐

Using Math

◆ How many 🐟 are left?

☐ − ☐ = ☐

🐟 are left.

4

Subtracting from 12

How many 🥚 are left?

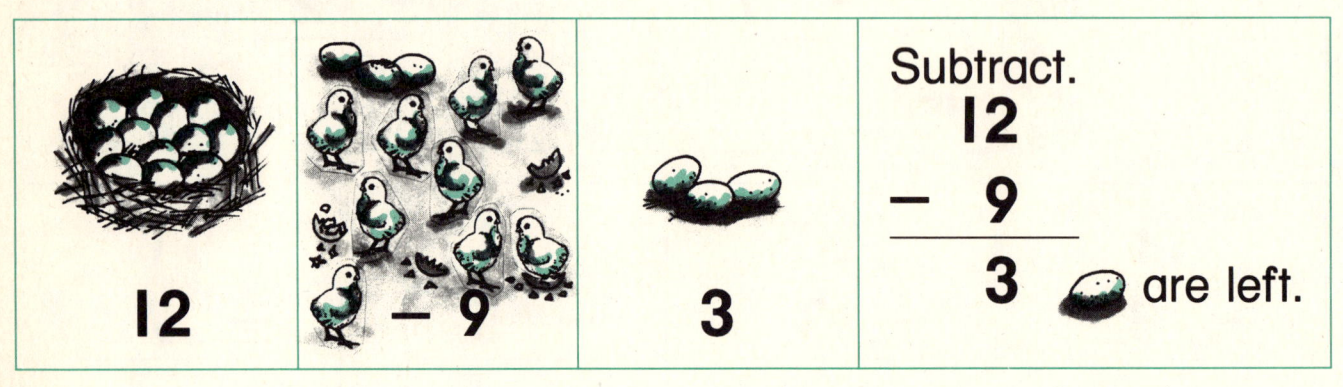

| 12 | − 9 | 3 | Subtract.
12
− 9
―――
3 🥚 are left. |

Guided Practice

◆ Subtract.

12
− 6
―――
[6]

12
− 7
―――
[ ]

12
− 3
―――
[ ]

12
− 8
―――
[ ]

104

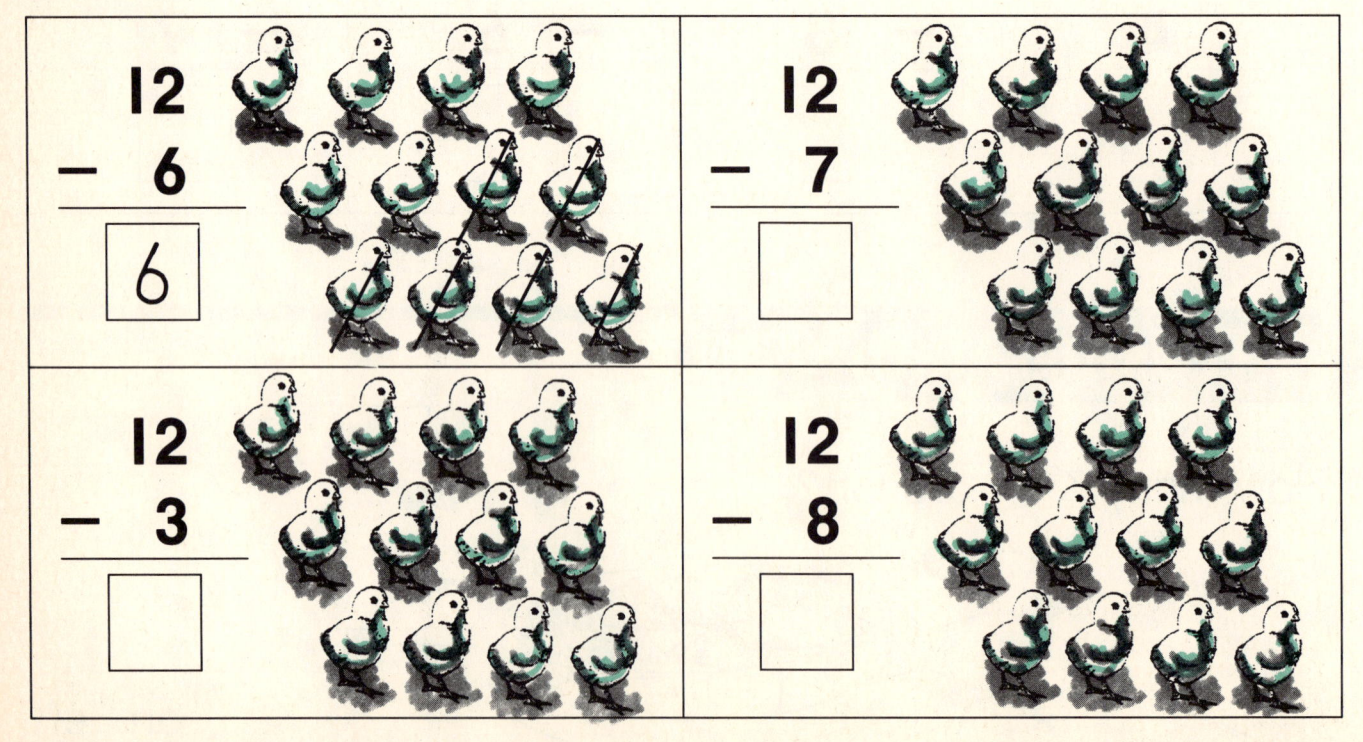

Practice

◆ Subtract.

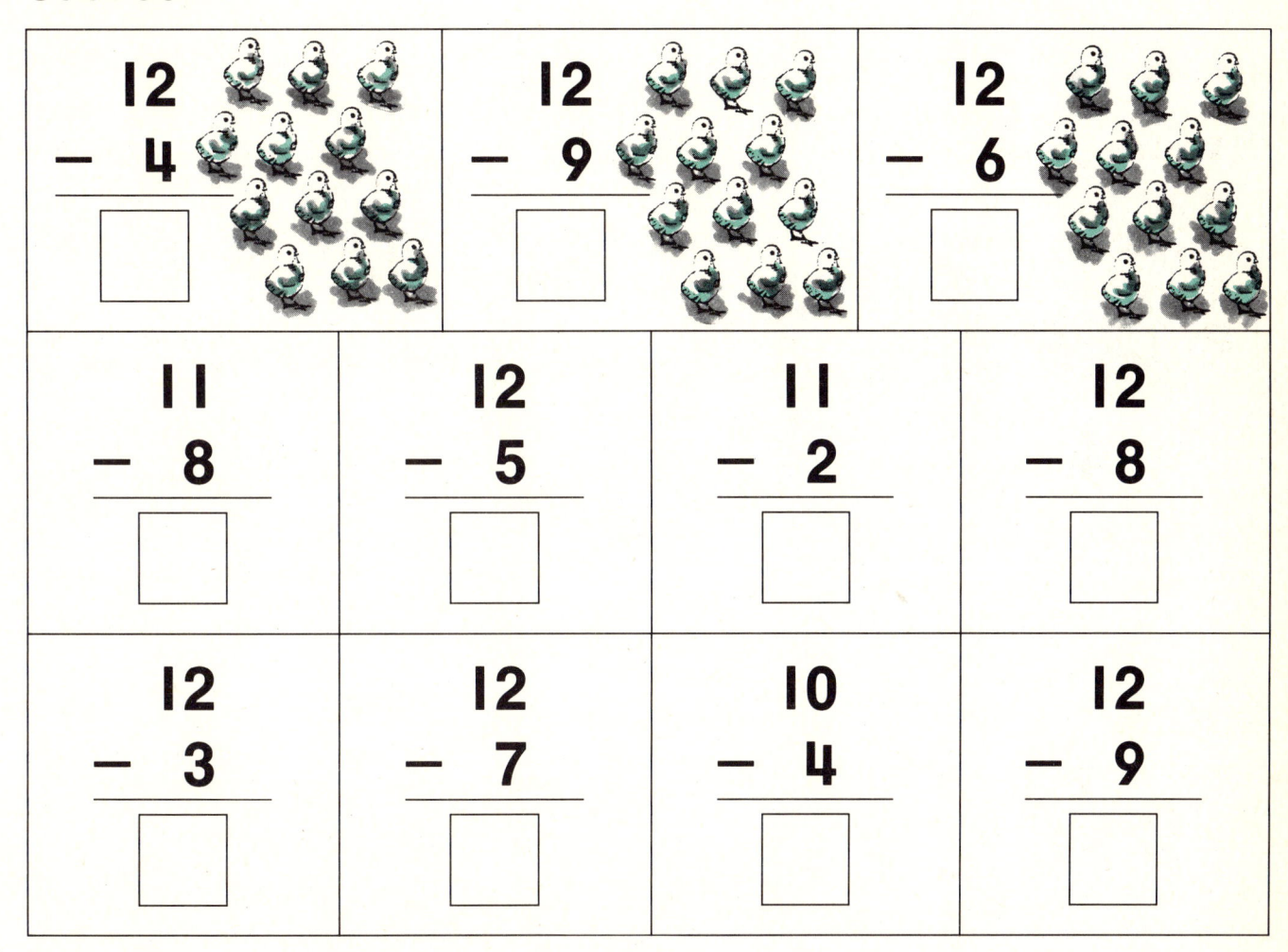

12 − 4 = ☐	12 − 9 = ☐	12 − 6 = ☐

11 − 8 = ☐	12 − 5 = ☐	11 − 2 = ☐	12 − 8 = ☐

12 − 3 = ☐	12 − 7 = ☐	10 − 4 = ☐	12 − 9 = ☐

Using Math

◆ How many 🥚 are left?

☐ − ☐ = ☐ 🥚 are left.

105

5

Ordinal Numbers

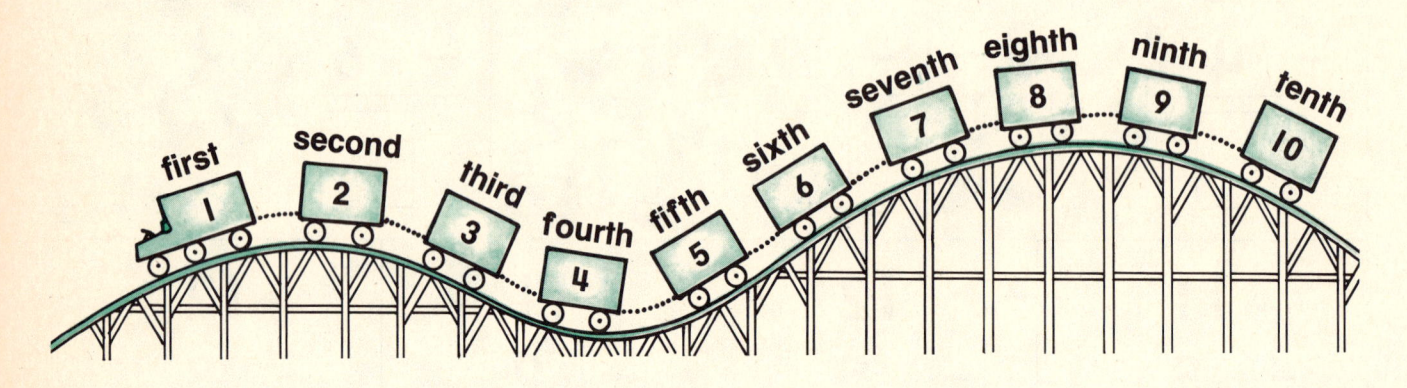

Guided Practice

◆ Color the correct 🚗 in each row.

fifth 🚩

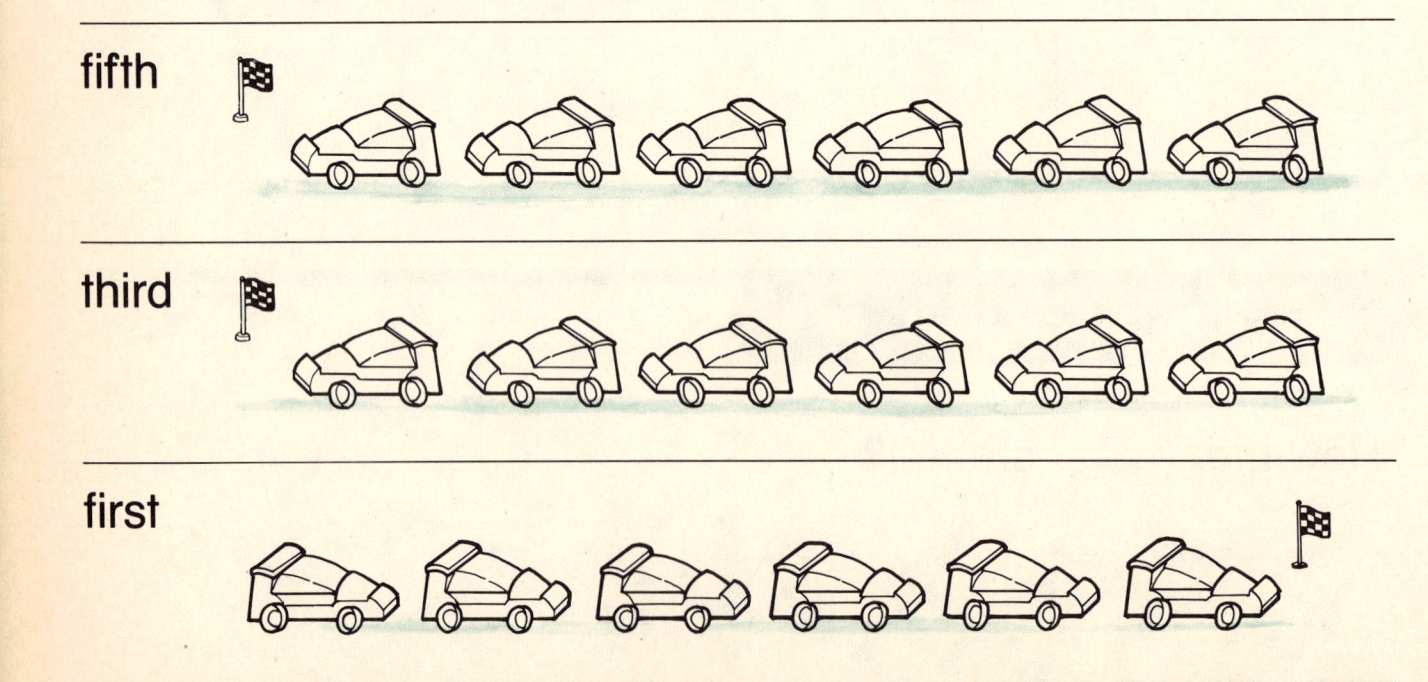

third 🚩

first   🚩

106

Practice

◆ Color the correct 🐴 in each row.

second

fourth

sixth

Problem Solving

◆ Write the numbers to complete a pattern.

| 24 | 26 | 28 | | | 34 | | | 40 | 42 |

| 47 | 49 | 51 | | 55 | 57 | | | | 65 |

| 10 | 15 | 20 | 25 | | | | 45 | | |

6

Comparing Numbers

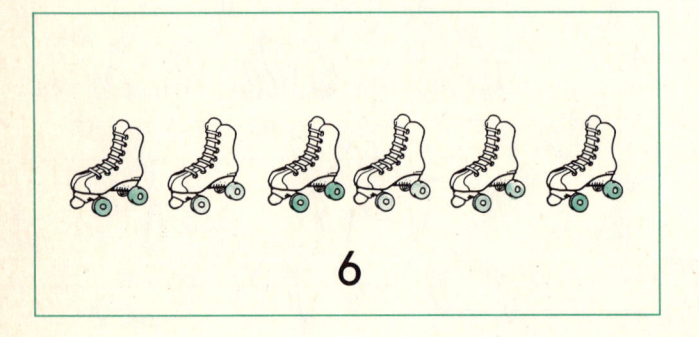

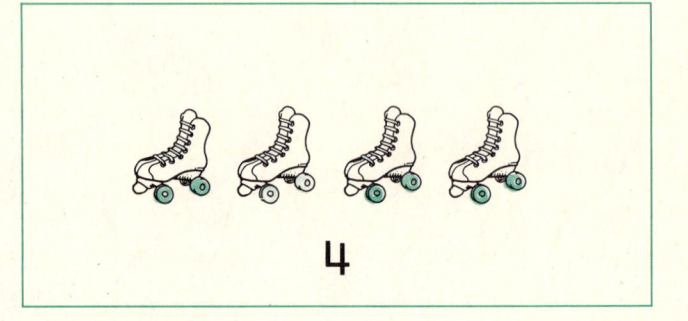

6

4

6 is **greater than** 4.
4 is **less than** 6.

Guided Practice

◆ Which is greater?

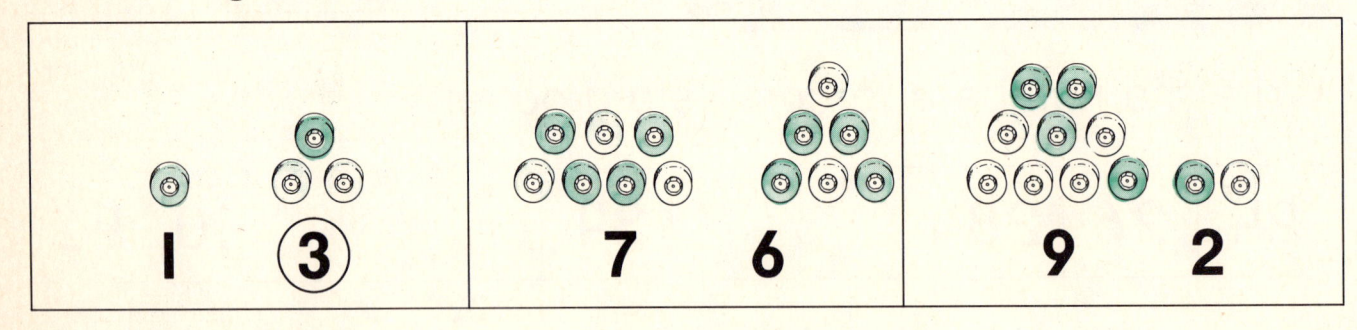

| 1 (3) | 7 6 | 9 2 |

◆ Which is less?

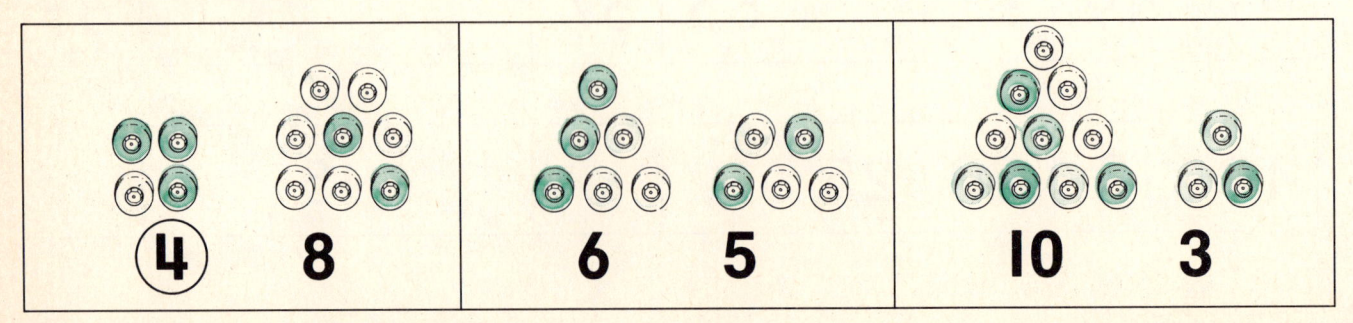

| (4) 8 | 6 5 | 10 3 |

Practice

◆ Which is greater?

2 4	1 5	6 3
12 7	8 4	11 10

◆ Which is less?

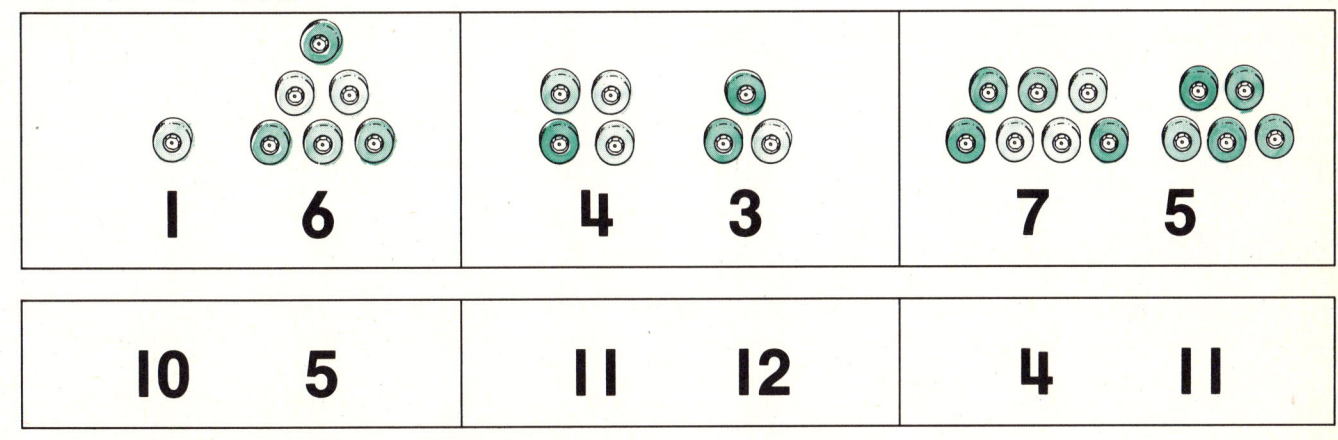

1 6	4 3	7 5
10 5	11 12	4 11

Using Math

◆ Jim has 7 🤖.
Pat has 5 🤖.

Write the numbers.

☐ is greater than ☐.

7

Counting Money

 1 penny 1 cent 1¢	 1 nickel 5 cents 5¢	 1 dime 10 cents 10¢	 1 quarter 25 cents 25¢

Guided Practice

◆ How much money?

(22¢) 28¢

8¢ 10¢

3¢ 30¢

28¢ 48¢

110

Practice

◆ Write how much money.

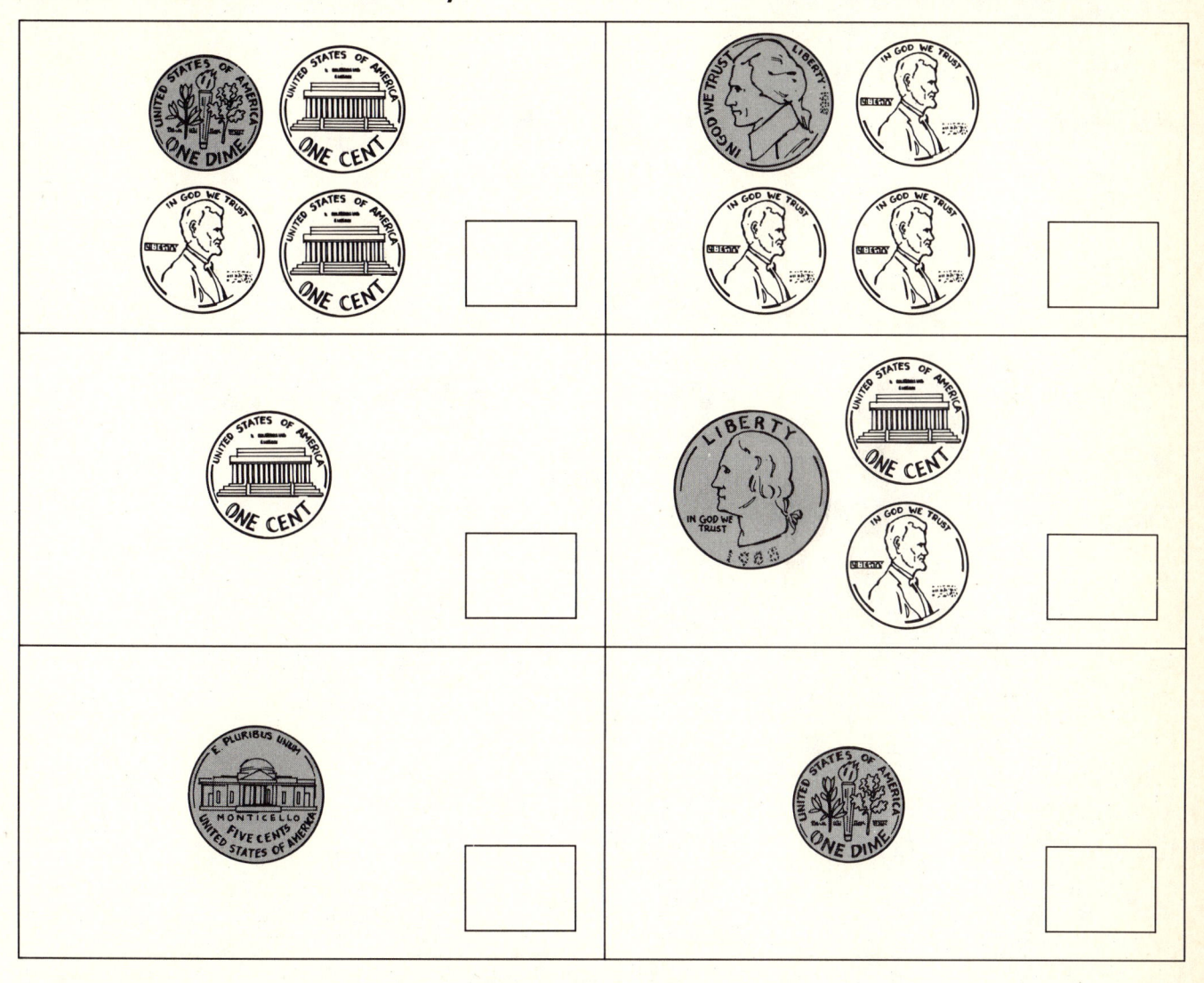

dime, penny, penny, penny ☐	nickel, penny, penny, penny ☐
penny ☐	quarter, penny, penny ☐
nickel ☐	dime ☐

Using Math

◆ Ring how much money.

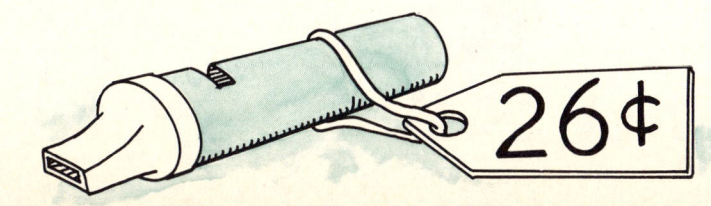

26¢

quarter, dime, penny, penny
quarter, penny, penny, penny

111

Problem Solving 8

Use a Graph

Albert went fishing.

He made a graph to show the fish he caught.

Albert's Fish

Kind of Fish

Guided Practice

◆ Look at the graph.
Write how many.

2

Practice

Manuel cleaned the art closet.
The graph shows what he found.

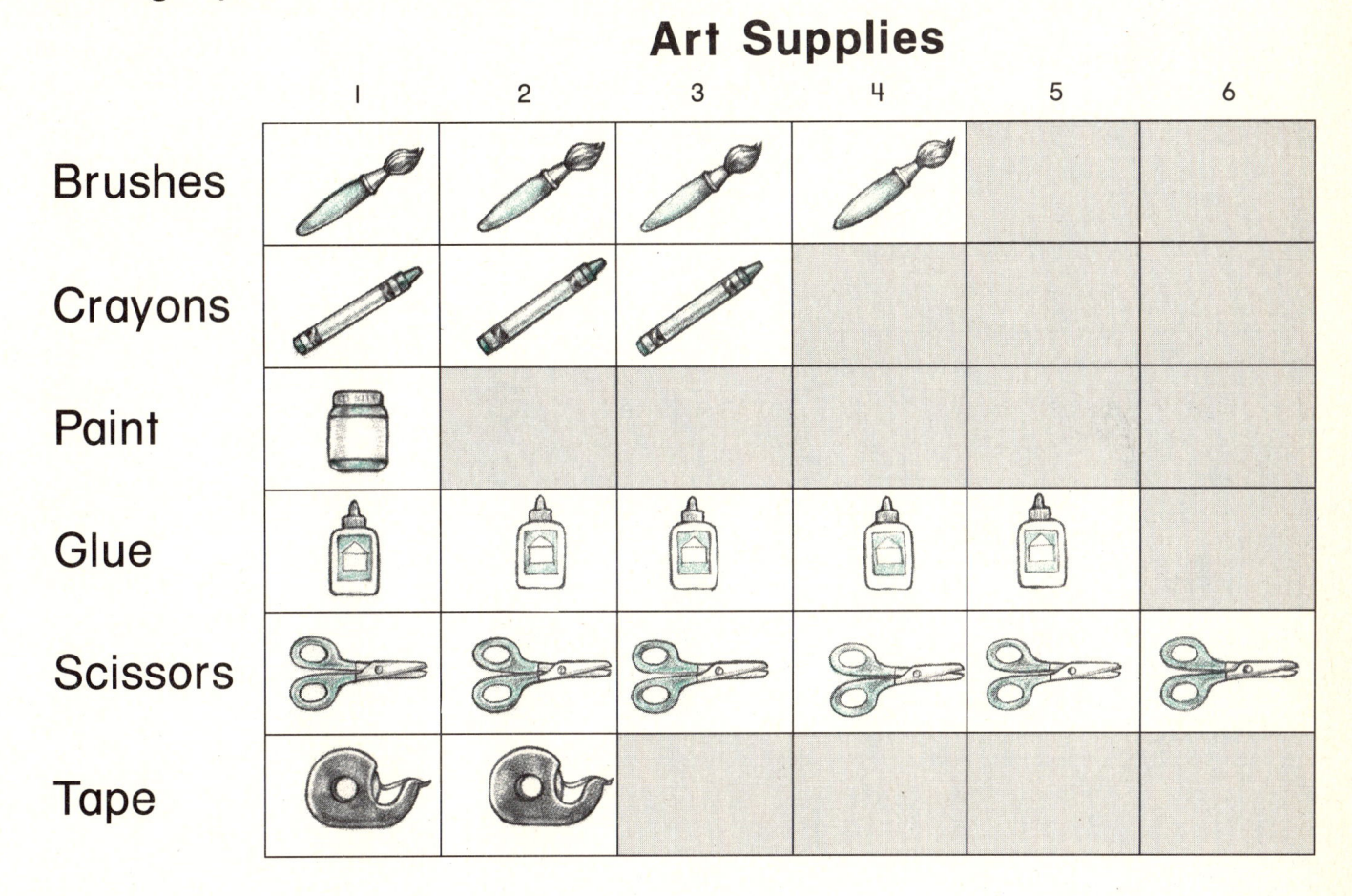

Art Supplies

	1	2	3	4	5	6
Brushes	🖌	🖌	🖌	🖌		
Crayons	✏	✏	✏			
Paint	🎨					
Glue	🧴	🧴	🧴	🧴	🧴	
Scissors	✂	✂	✂	✂	✂	✂
Tape	📼	📼				

◆ Look at the graph. Write how many.

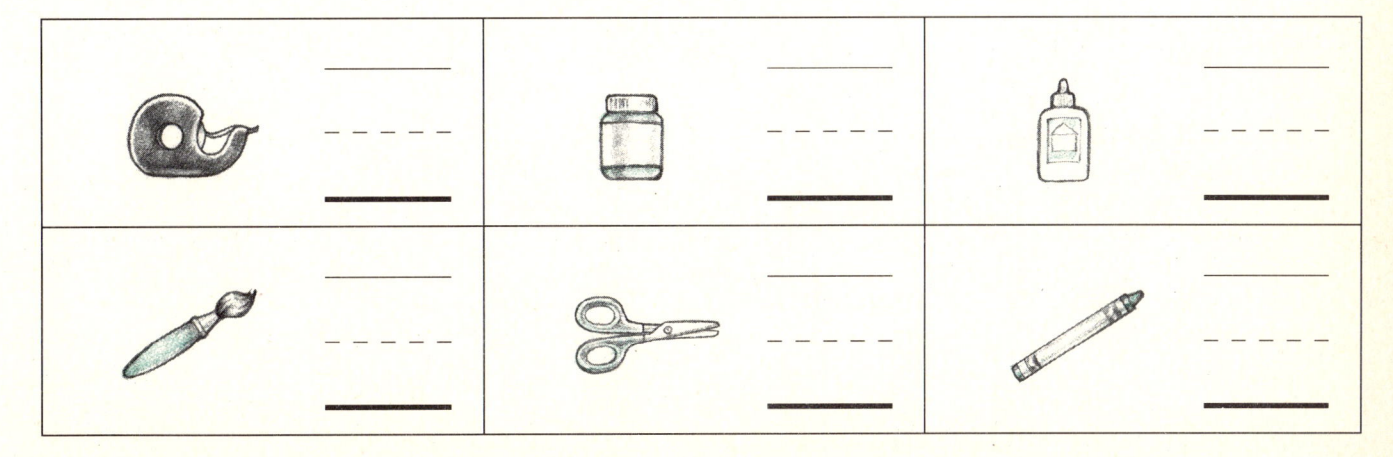

| tape ___ | paint ___ | glue ___ |
| brush ___ | scissors ___ | crayon ___ |

113

Review

◆ Add.

pages 98–99			
9 + 2	5 + 6	8 + 3	7 + 4

pages 100–101			
6 + 6	7 + 5	3 + 9	4 + 8

◆ Subtract.

pages 102–103			
11 − 9	11 − 3	11 − 6	11 − 8

pages 104–105			
12 − 4	12 − 6	12 − 3	12 − 7

CHAPTER 5

◆ **Color the correct** 🚗.
pages 106–107

sixth

third

◆ **Which is greater?**
pages 108–109

| 12 6 | 5 8 | 4 1 |

◆ **Which is less?**

| 10 3 | 9 11 | 7 5 |

◆ **Write how much money.**
pages 110–111

Review

CHAPTER 5

Chu opened a jar of mixed nuts.
He made a graph to show what was in the jar.

Mixed Nuts in a Jar

◆ Look at the graph.
Write how many.

pages 112–113

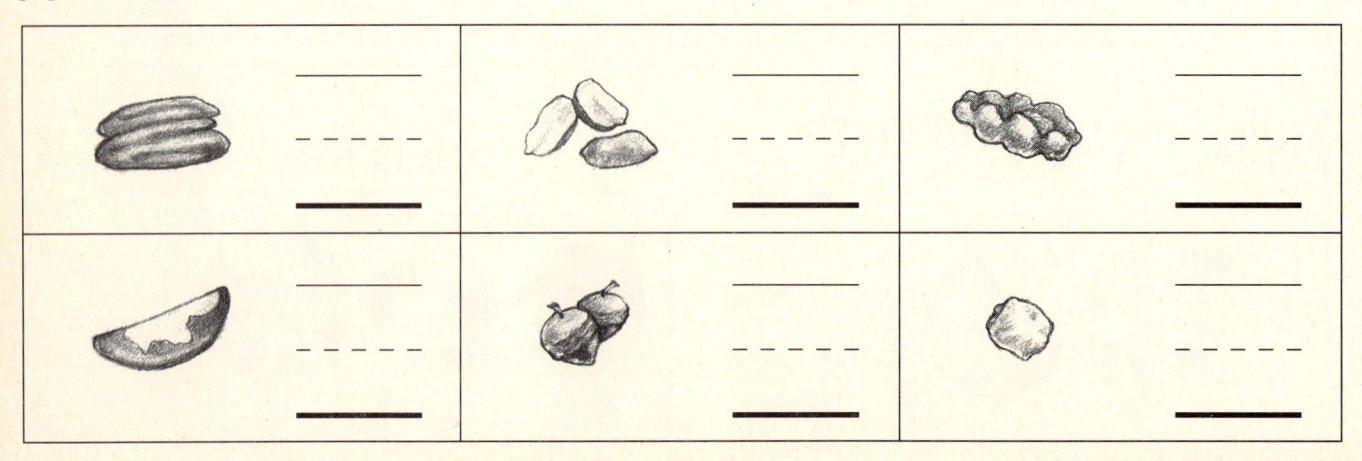

Test

CHAPTER 5

◆ Add.

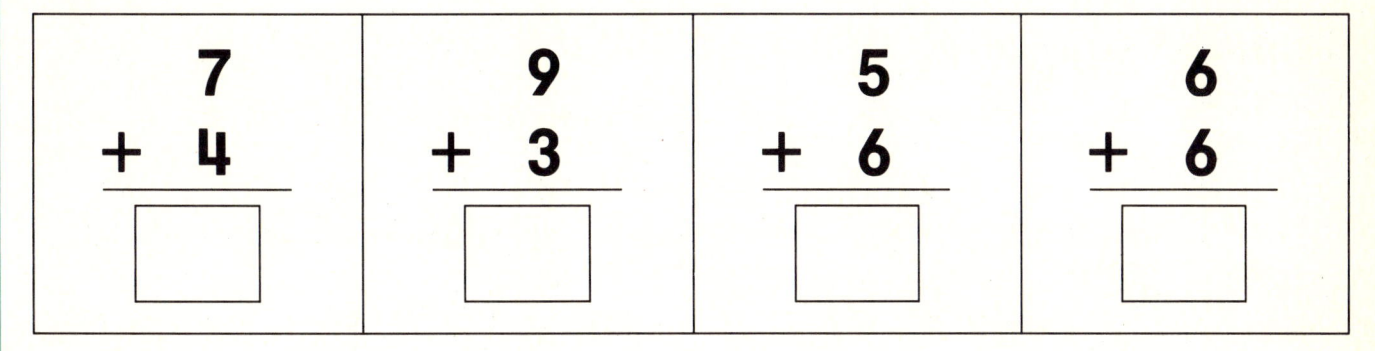

| 7 + 4 = ☐ | 9 + 3 = ☐ | 5 + 6 = ☐ | 6 + 6 = ☐ |

◆ Subtract.

| 11 − 5 = ☐ | 12 − 4 = ☐ | 11 − 7 = ☐ | 12 − 7 = ☐ |

◆ Color the second 🚗.

◆ Which is greater?   9   3   Which is less?   5   8

◆ Write how much money.

☐

117

Test

CHAPTER 5

Ben collects shells.
He made a graph to show how many shells he has.

Ben's Shells

Kind of Shell

◆ Look at the graph.
Write how many.

118

Name _____

CHAPTER 6

Adding and Subtracting 2-Digit Numbers

About how many oranges are in one bag?
About how many students are in your class?
Is one bag of oranges enough for your class?
How do you know?

119

1

Adding Ones and Tens

How many in all?

23 + 6

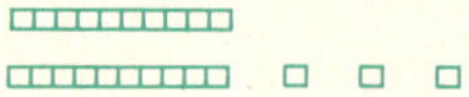

Add.

23
+ 6

Step 1 Add the ones.

tens	ones
2	3
+	6
	9

Step 2 Add the tens.

tens	ones
2	3
+ 0	6
2	9

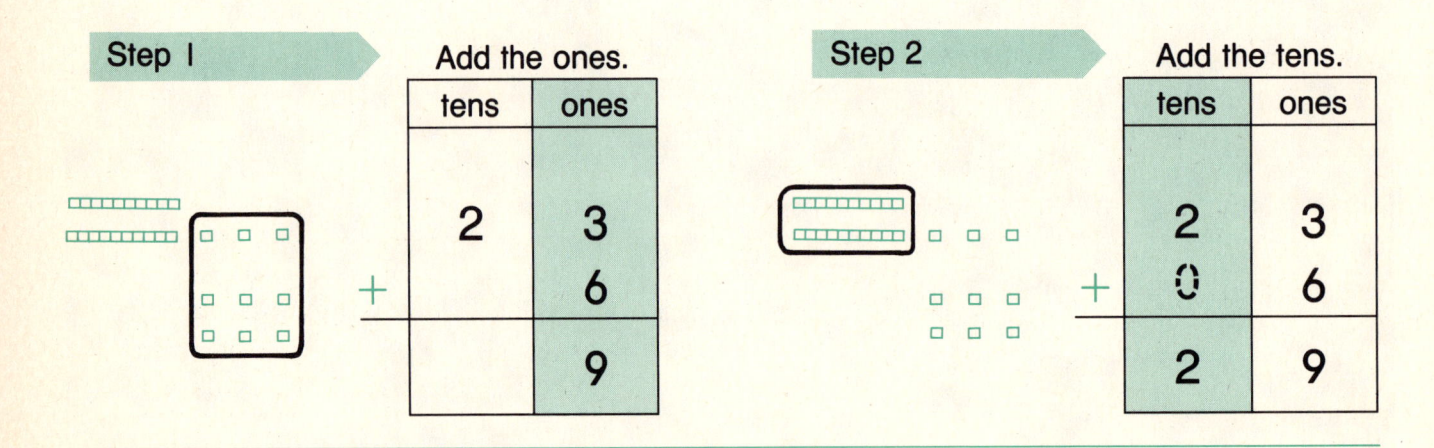

Guided Practice

◆ Add.

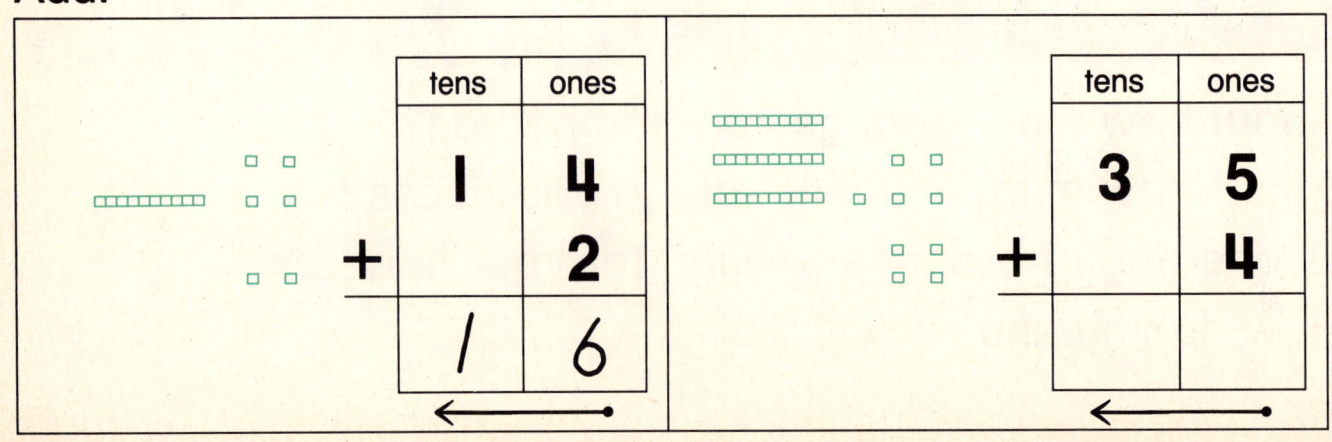

tens	ones
1	4
+	2
1	6

tens	ones
3	5
+	4

Practice

◆ Add.

	tens	ones
	3	3
+		3

	tens	ones
	1	1
+		4

```
  41        95        64        51
+  6      +  4      +  2      + 1
 ___       ___       ___       ___
[   ]     [   ]     [   ]     [   ]

  78        51        83        22
+  1      +  4      +  4      +  5
 ___       ___       ___       ___
[   ]     [   ]     [   ]     [   ]
```

Using Math

◆ How much money in all?

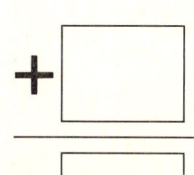

[ ]
+ [ ]
[ ]

121

2

Adding Two 2-Digit Numbers

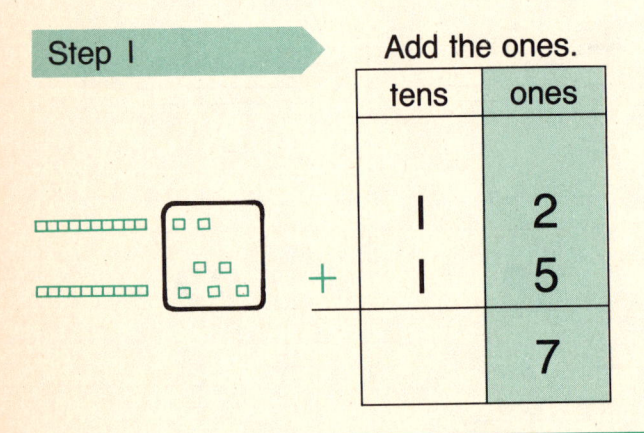

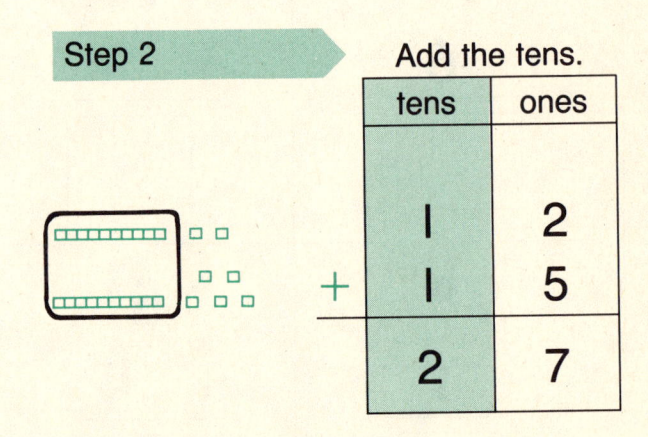

How many in all?

12 + 15

Add.

12
+ 15

Step 1 Add the ones.

tens	ones
1	2
+ 1	5
	7

Step 2 Add the tens.

tens	ones
1	2
+ 1	5
2	7

Guided Practice

◆ Add.

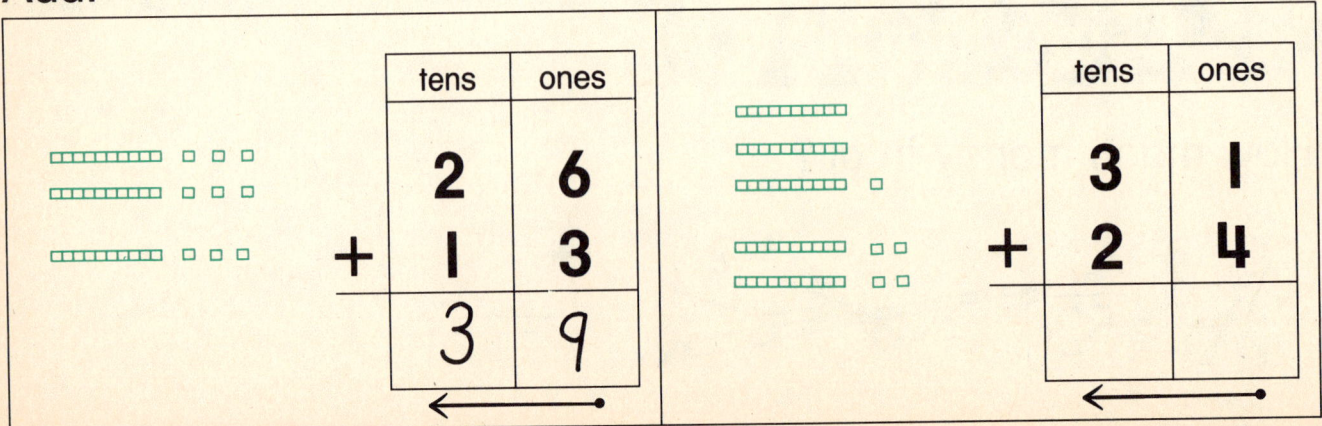

tens	ones
2	6
+ 1	3
3	9

tens	ones
3	1
+ 2	4

122

Practice

◆ Add.

	tens	ones
	2	3
+	2	2

	tens	ones
	2	3
+	1	3

64
+ 35

57
+ 21

23
+ 41

32
+ 21

53
+ 44

43
+ 42

81
+ 16

15
+ 11

Using Math

◆ How much money in all?

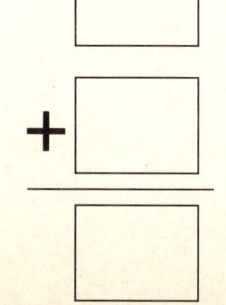

75¢
24¢

☐
+ ☐
―――
☐

123

3

Adding Tens

How many in all?

50 + 30

Add.

50
+ 30

Step 1 — Add the ones.

tens	ones
5	0
+ 3	0
	0

Step 2 — Add the tens.

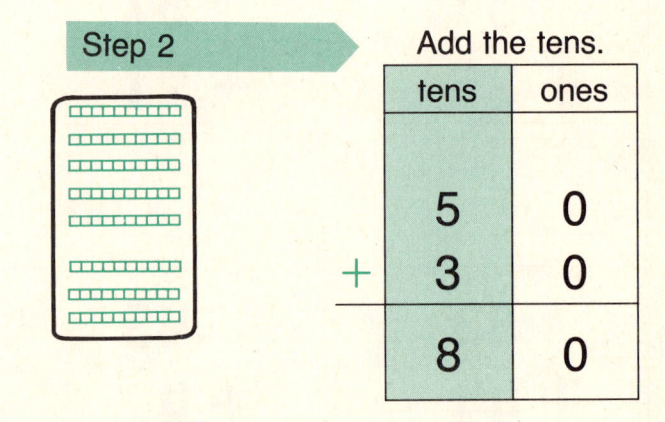

tens	ones
5	0
+ 3	0
8	0

Guided Practice

◆ Add.

tens	ones
3	0
+ 2	0
5	0

tens	ones
2	0
+ 1	0

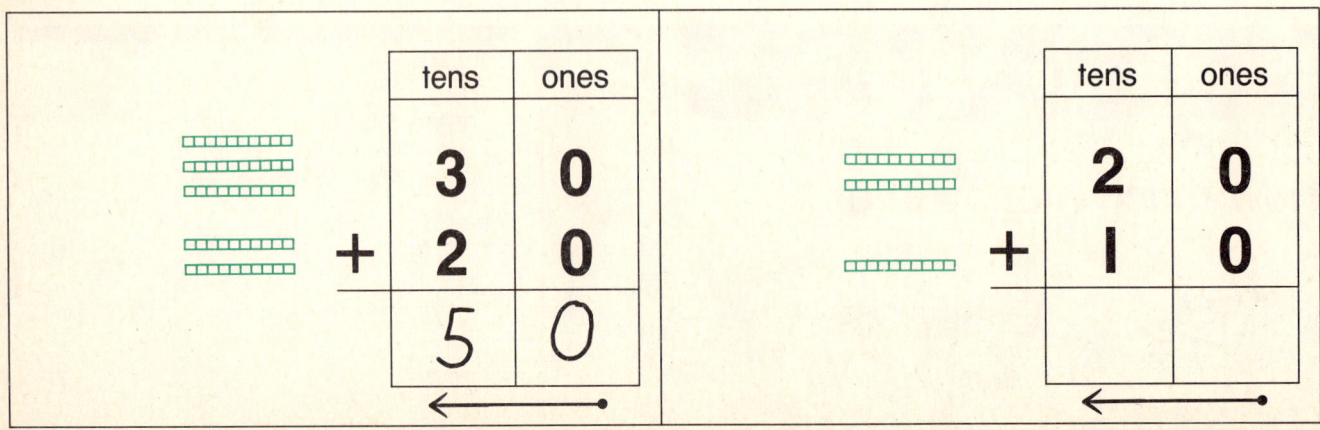

124

Practice

◆ Add.

	tens	ones
	3	0
+	3	0

	tens	ones
	1	0
+	1	0

60 + 10	50 + 40	60 + 30	10 + 30

40 + 40	50 + 20	10 + 40	20 + 20

Using Math

◆ How much money in all?

125

4

Subtracting Ones and Tens

How many are left?

17 − 5

Subtract.

17
− 5

Step 1 Subtract the ones.

tens	ones
1	7
	5
	2

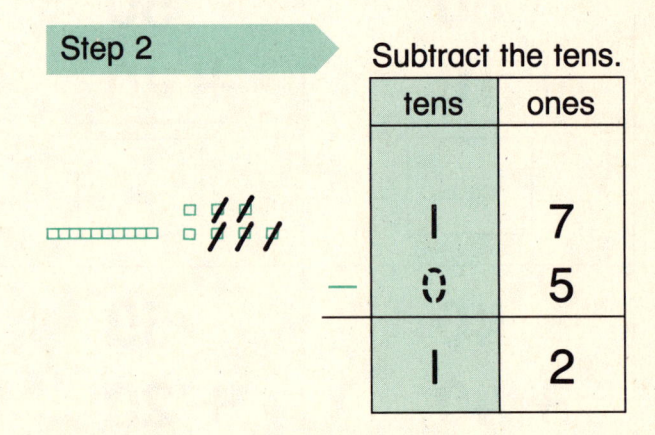

Step 2 Subtract the tens.

tens	ones
1	7
0	5
1	2

Guided Practice

◆ Subtract.

tens	ones
2	5
	4
2	1

tens	ones
1	9
	8

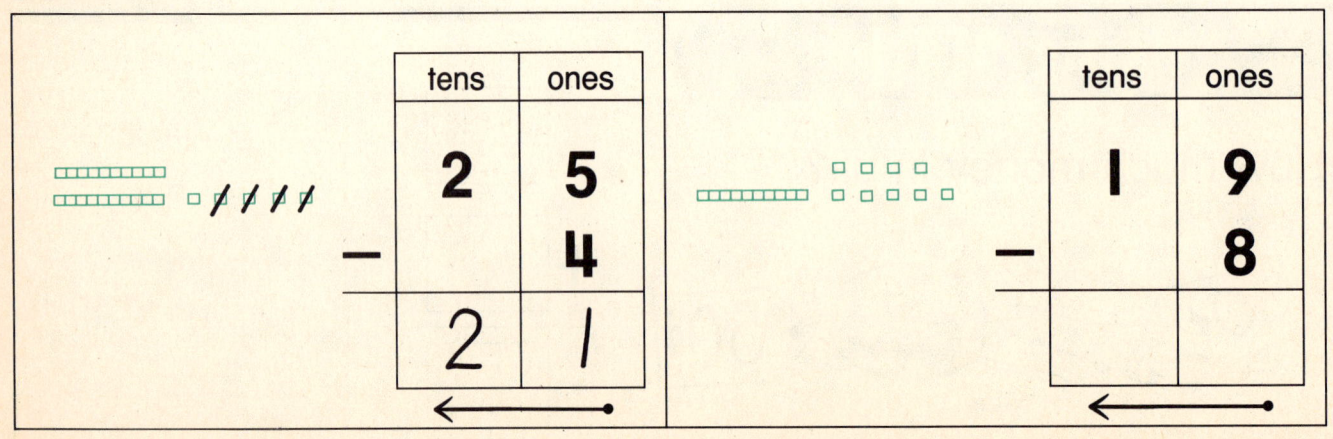

126

Practice

◆ Subtract.

tens	ones
4	4
	3

tens	ones
1	3
	1

98   65   87   33
− 4   − 2   − 5   − 2

28   36   52   11
− 3   − 6   − 1   − 1

Using Math

◆ How much money is left?

You have

You buy

127

5

Subtracting Two 2-Digit Numbers

How many are left?

25 − 13

Subtract.

25
− 13

Step 1 — Subtract the ones.

tens	ones
2	5
− 1	3
	2

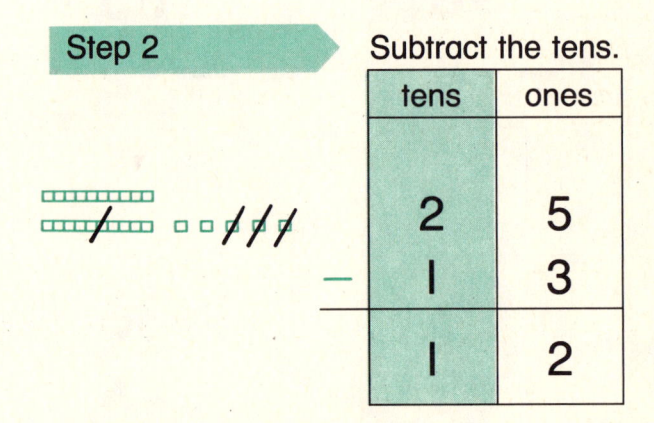

Step 2 — Subtract the tens.

tens	ones
2	5
− 1	3
1	2

Guided Practice

◆ Subtract.

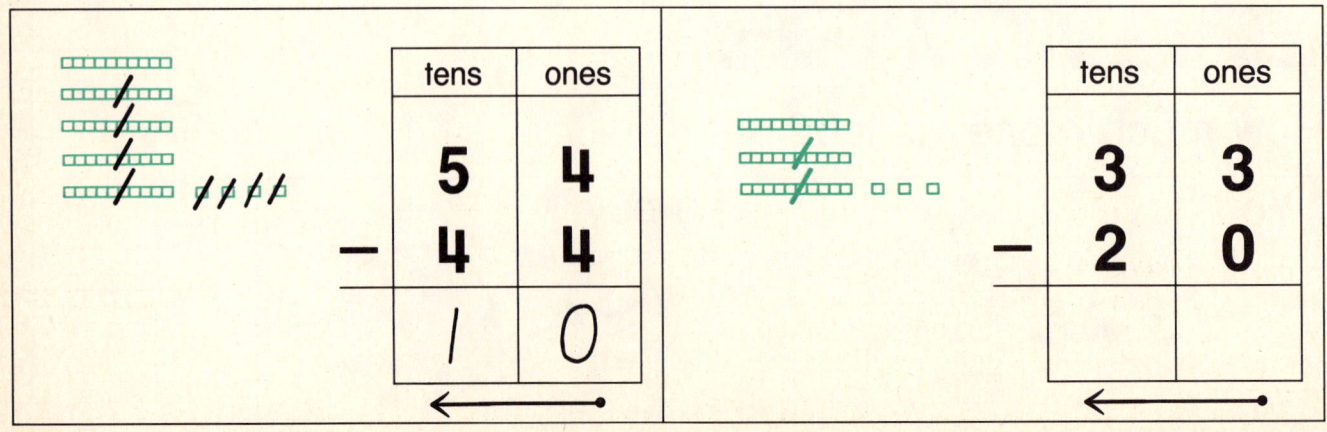

tens	ones
5	4
− 4	4
1	0

tens	ones
3	3
− 2	0

128

Practice

◆ Subtract.

	tens	ones
	4	4
−	1	4

	tens	ones
	3	5
−	1	1

```
  67        59        93        45
− 22      − 17      − 42      − 12
```

```
  88        73        78        26
− 62      − 21      − 35      − 12
```

Using Math

◆ How much money is left?

You have (quarter) You buy (apple) 12¢

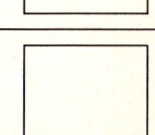

129

6

Subtracting Tens

How many are left?   Subtract.

50 − 20   50
                − 20

Step 1 Subtract the ones.

tens	ones
5	0
− 2	0
	0

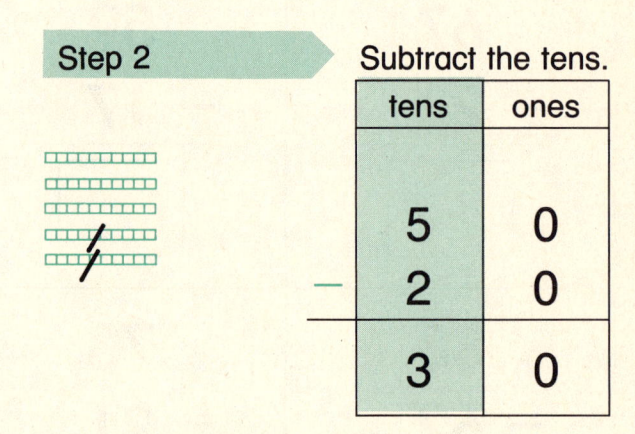

Step 2 Subtract the tens.

tens	ones
5	0
− 2	0
3	0

Guided Practice

◆ Subtract.

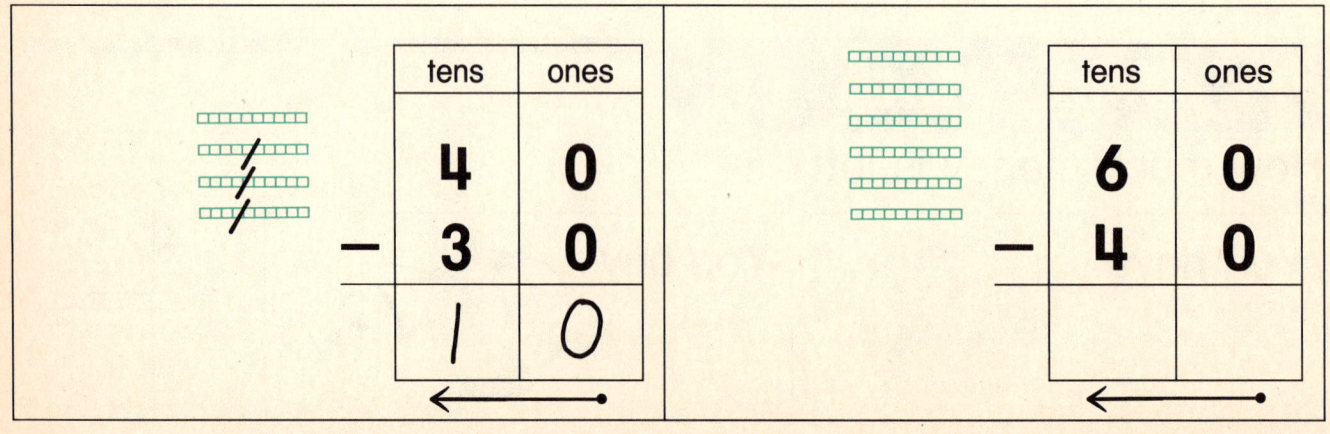

tens	ones
4	0
− 3	0
1	0

tens	ones
6	0
− 4	0

Practice

◆ Subtract.

	tens	ones
	6	0
−	1	0

	tens	ones
	4	0
−	1	0

90 − 30	60 − 20	70 − 40	30 − 20

50 − 40	10 − 10	80 − 30	20 − 10

Problem Solving

Lena made a graph to show how many pets she has.

◆ Write how many.

Lena's Pets

131

7

Counting Money

 penny	 nickel	 dime	 quarter
1¢	5¢	10¢	25¢

Guided Practice

◆ How much money?

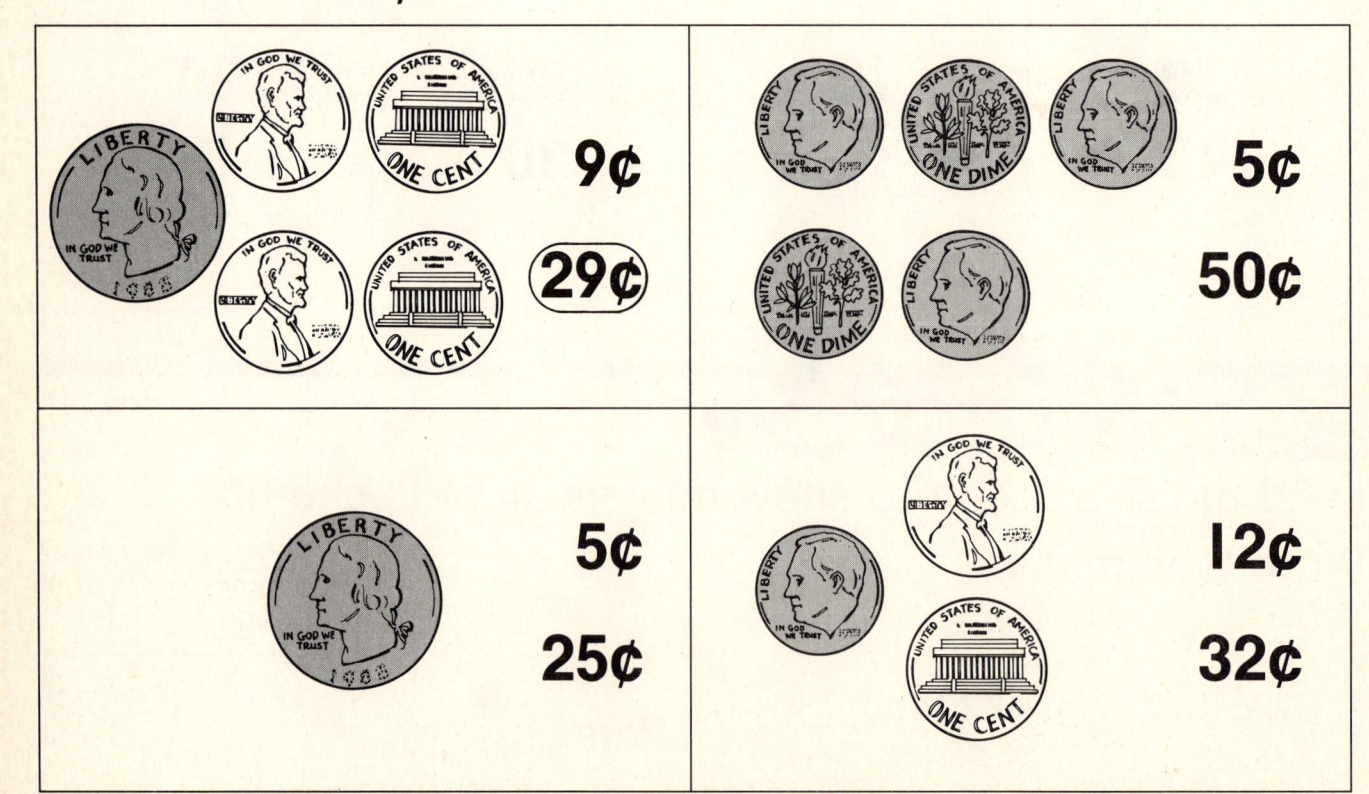

9¢
(29¢)

5¢
50¢

5¢
25¢

12¢
32¢

132

Practice

◆ Write how much money.

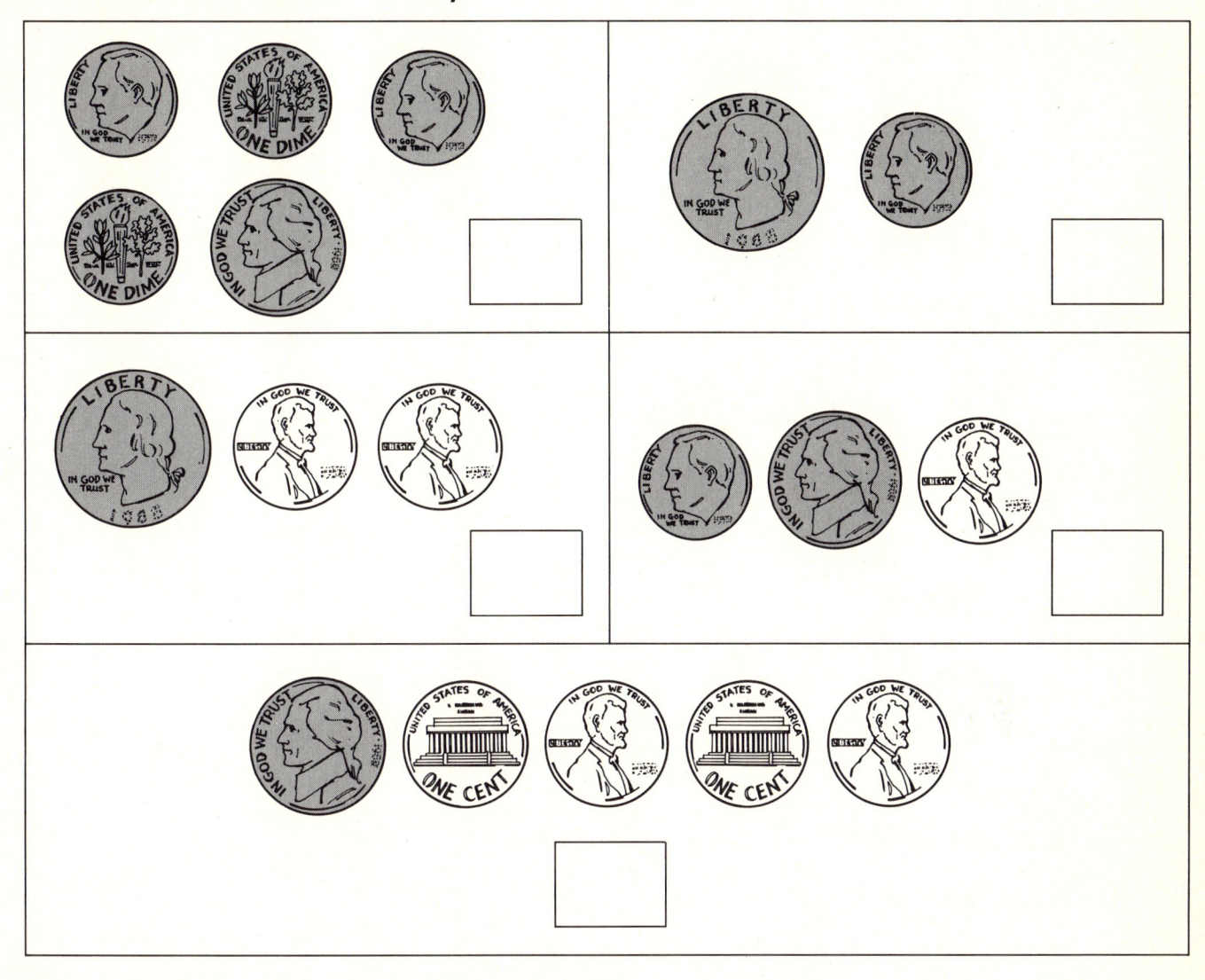

3 dimes, 1 nickel (illustrated) ☐	2 quarters (illustrated) ☐
1 quarter, 2 pennies (illustrated) ☐	1 dime, 1 nickel, 1 penny (illustrated) ☐
1 nickel, 4 pennies (illustrated) ☐	

Using Math

◆ Ring how much money.

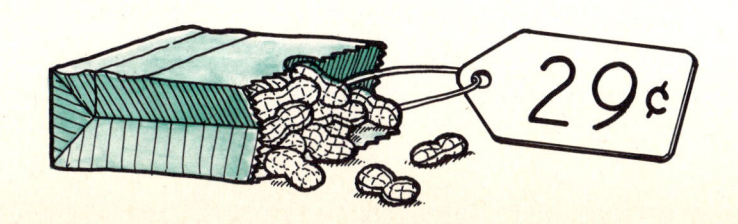

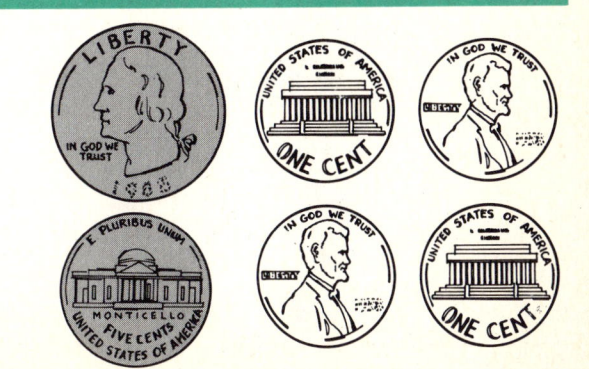

Problem Solving 8

Use a Graph

Favorite Sports

Ms. Davis asked each student in her class to name his or her favorite sport. She used their answers to make this graph.

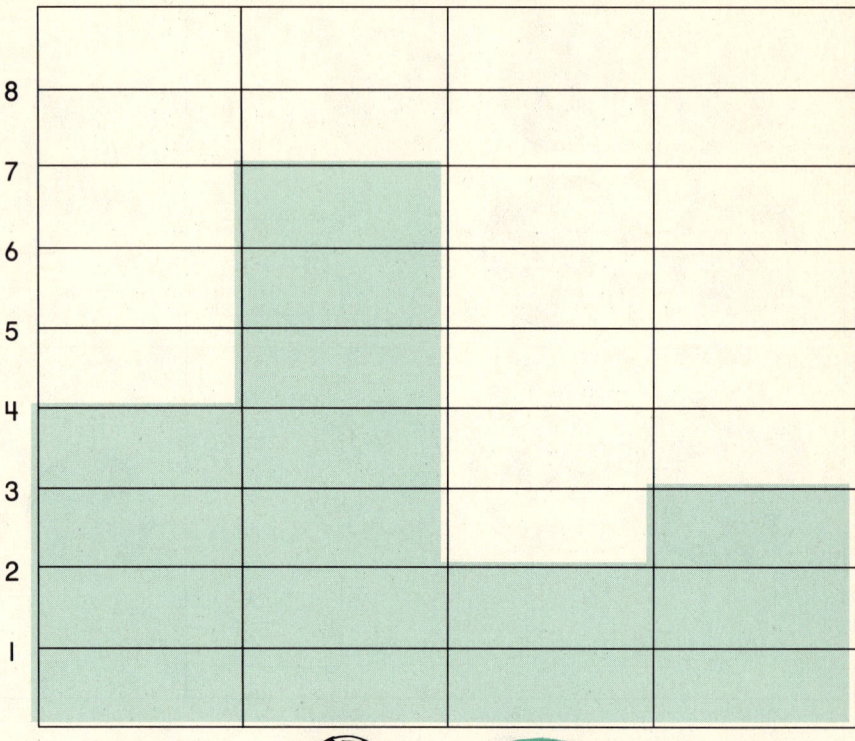

Guided Practice

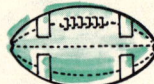

◆ Look at the graph.
Write how many like to play each sport.

134

Practice

Ron plays a drum in a marching band. He made a graph of the instruments in the band.

Band Instruments

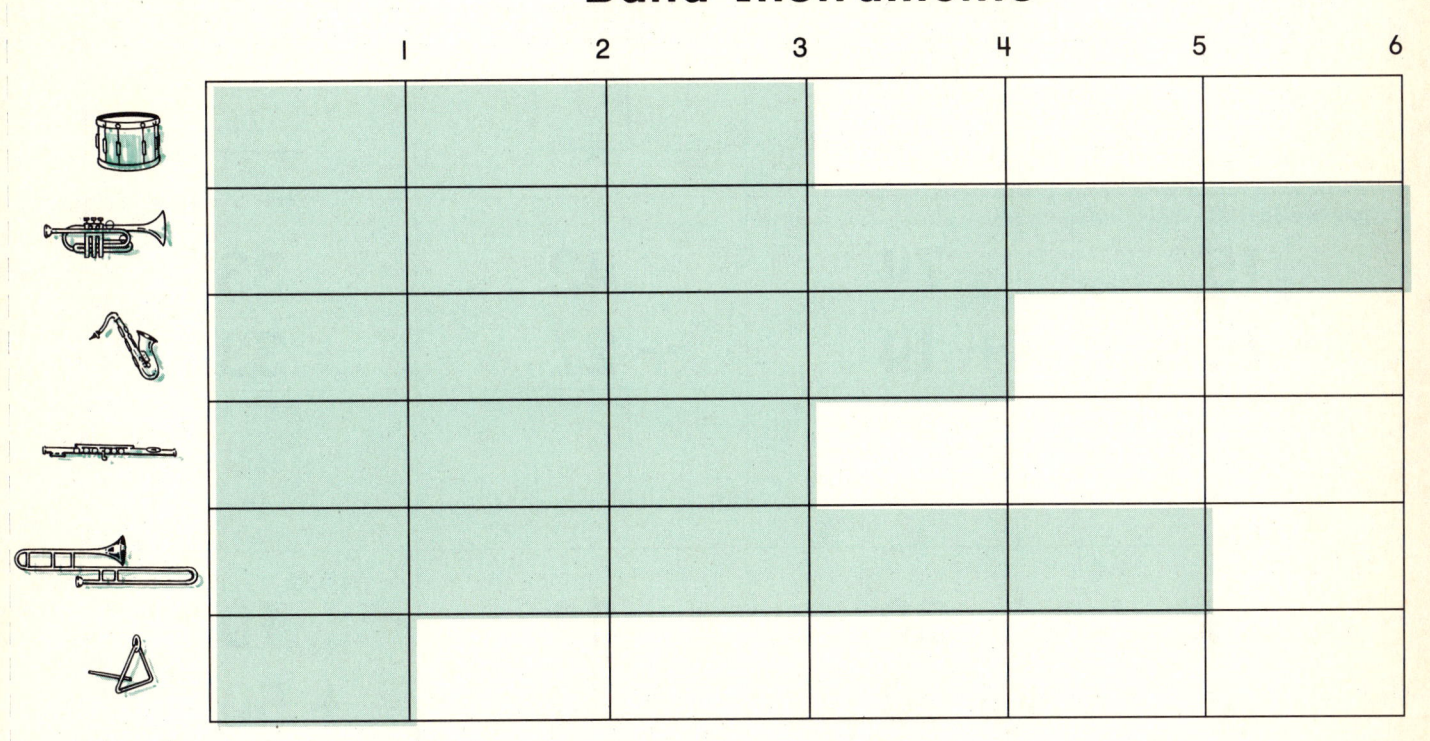

	1	2	3	4	5	6
drum	■	■	■			
trumpet	■	■	■	■	■	■
saxophone	■	■	■	■		
flute	■	■	■			
trombone	■	■	■	■	■	
triangle	■					

◆ Look at the graph. Write how many of each.

| triangle ___ | drum ___ | saxophone ___ |
| flute ___ | trumpet ___ | trombone ___ |

135

Review

◆ Add.

pages 120–121

| 22 + 6 ☐ | 93 + 4 ☐ | 51 + 3 ☐ | 11 + 6 ☐ |

pages 122–123

| 15 + 14 ☐ | 74 + 14 ☐ | 42 + 27 ☐ | 33 + 33 ☐ |

pages 124–125

| 20 + 10 ☐ | 30 + 20 ☐ | 50 + 40 ☐ | 10 + 50 ☐ |

◆ Subtract.

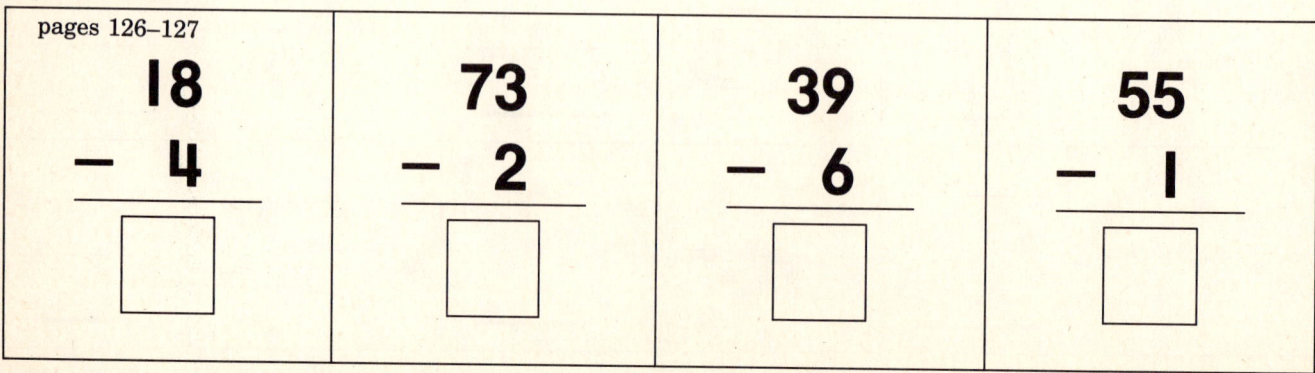

pages 126–127

| 18 − 4 ☐ | 73 − 2 ☐ | 39 − 6 ☐ | 55 − 1 ☐ |

CHAPTER 6

◆ Subtract.

pages 128–129

| 34 − 11 | 67 − 32 | 86 − 46 | 95 − 12 |

pages 130–131

| 50 − 40 | 80 − 30 | 20 − 20 | 70 − 40 |

◆ Write how much money.
pages 132–133

Review

CHAPTER 6

Mr. Walker asked his students to name their favorite bicycle color. He made a graph to show what they said.

Favorite Colors

	Red	Blue	Black	Green	Yellow	Purple
8						
7	■					
6	■					
5	■	■				
4	■	■				
3	■	■	■	■		
2	■	■	■	■	■	
1	■	■	■	■	■	■

◆ Look at the graph. Write how many of each.

pages 134–135

| Yellow ___ | Blue ___ | Purple ___ |
| Black ___ | Red ___ | Green ___ |

Test

CHAPTER 6

◆ Add.

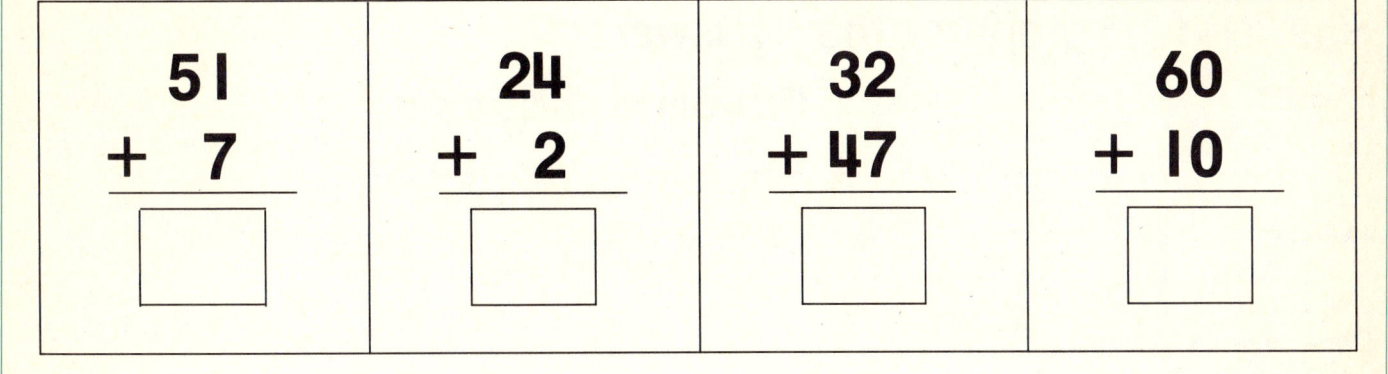

51	24	32	60
+ 7	+ 2	+47	+10

◆ Subtract.

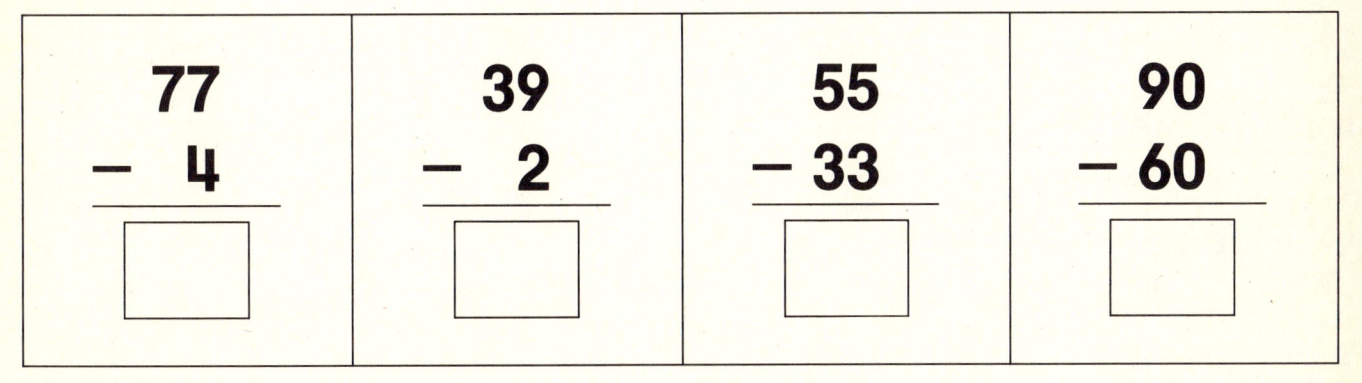

77	39	55	90
− 4	− 2	−33	−60

◆ Write how much money.

139

Test

CHAPTER 6

Ann asked her friends to name their favorite snack. She made a graph of their answers.

Favorite Snacks

	1	2	3	4	5	6	7	8
Apple	▓	▓	▓	▓	▓			
Popcorn	▓	▓	▓	▓	▓	▓	▓	▓
Peanuts	▓	▓	▓	▓				
Muffin	▓	▓						
Cookies	▓	▓	▓	▓	▓	▓		
Almonds	▓							

◆ Look at the graph. Write how many of each.

Peanuts _____	Almonds _____	Popcorn _____
Muffin _____	Apple _____	Cookies _____

140

Cumulative Review — CHAPTER 4

◆ How many?

pages 76–79

27 = ☐ tens ☐ ones

32 = ☐ tens ☐ ones

pages 80–83

tens	ones

= ☐

tens	ones

= ☐

pages 84–85

tens	ones

= ☐

tens	ones

= ☐

◆ Write how much money.

pages 88–89

141

◆ Write the numbers to complete a pattern.
pages 90–91

| 8 | 10 | 12 | | | | 20 | | 24 | |

| 37 | 39 | | 43 | | | 49 | 51 | | |

| 6 | 7 | 8 | | | 11 | | | | 15 |

| 25 | 30 | 35 | | | | 55 | | | |

| | 20 | | 40 | | 60 | | 80 | | |

| 46 | 47 | 48 | 49 | | | | | | |

◆ Use numbers to make a pattern of your own.

| | | | | | | | | | |

142

CHAPTER 5

◆ Add.

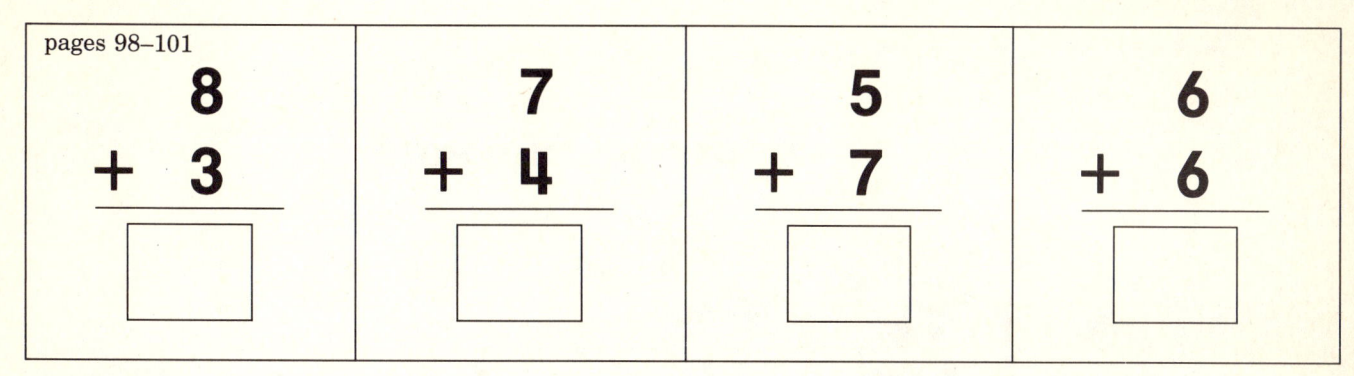

pages 98–101

| 8 | 7 | 5 | 6 |
|+ 3 | + 4 | + 7 | + 6 |

◆ Subtract.

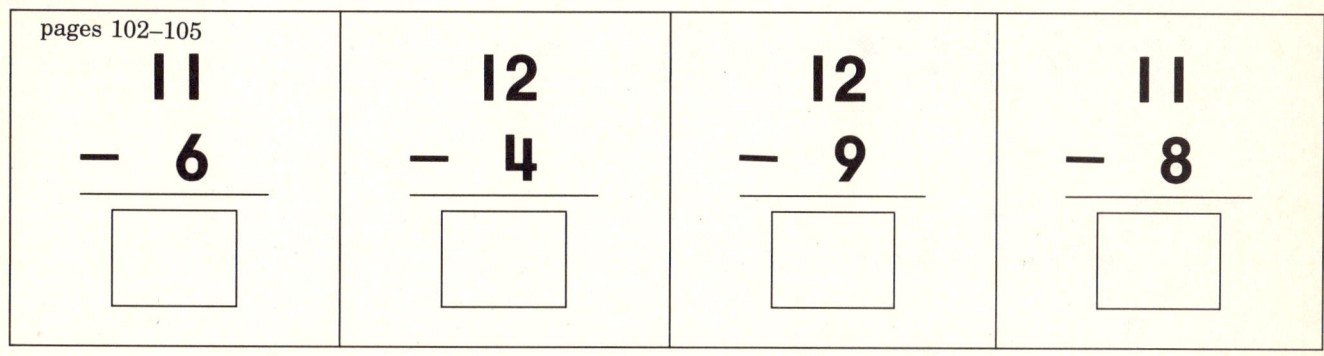

pages 102–105

| 11 | 12 | 12 | 11 |
|− 6 | − 4 | − 9 | − 8 |

◆ Mark the fourth 🐕 .

pages 106–107

pages 108–109

◆ Which is greater?   4   6   Which is less?   12   9

pages 110–111

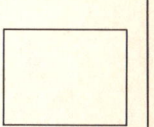

◆ Write how much money.

143

Eve counted insects in the park.
She made a graph to show what she saw.

Insects in the Park

Kind of Insect

◆ Look at the graph.
Write how many of each.

pages 112–113

144

CHAPTER 6

◆ Add.

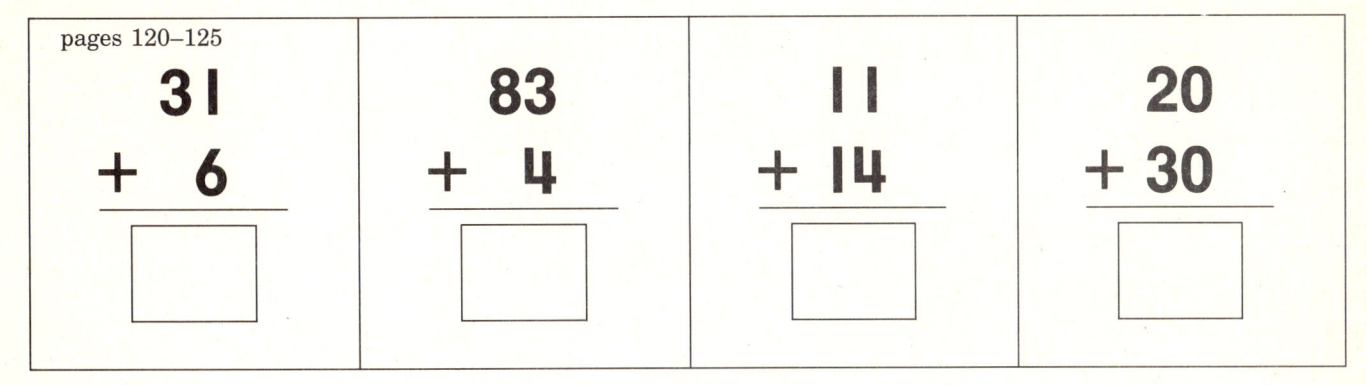

pages 120–125

| 31 | 83 | 11 | 20 |
|+ 6|+ 4|+14|+30|

◆ Subtract.

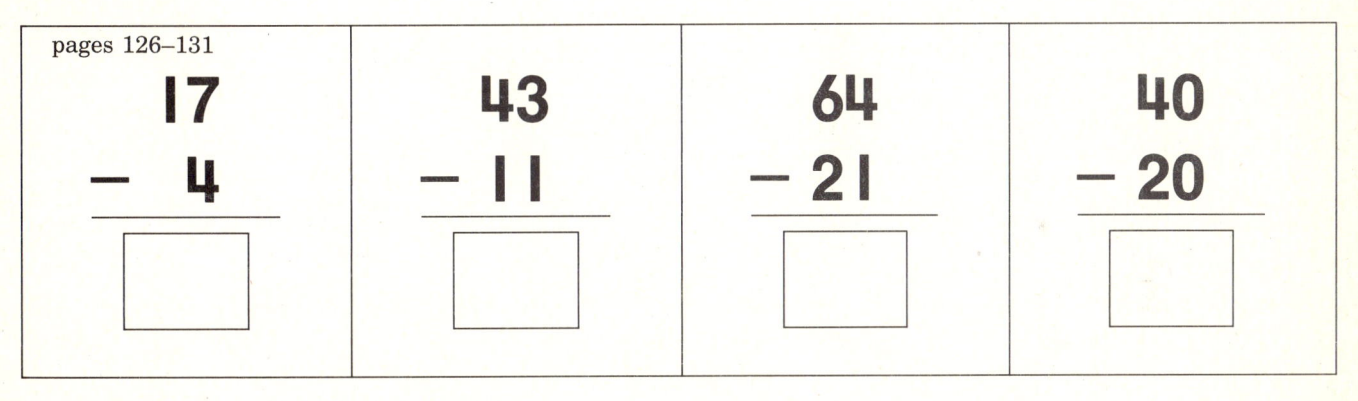

pages 126–131

| 17 | 43 | 64 | 40 |
|− 4|−11|−21|−20|

◆ Write how much money.
pages 132–133

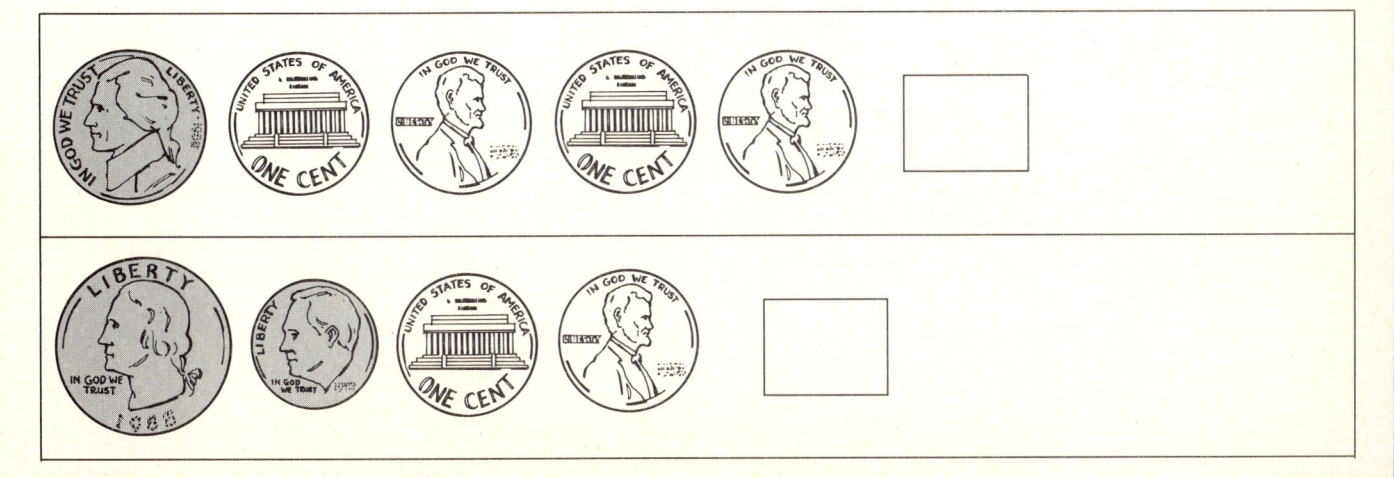

145

Ms. Jones' students all have birthdays in the summer and fall.
She made a graph to show the number of birthdays in each month.

The Number of Birthdays Each Month

June	2
July	1
August	5
September	7
October	3
November	3

◆ Look at the graph. Write how many.
pages 134–135

November _3_	September _7_	July _1_
June _2_	October _3_	August _5_

146

Extra Practice

CHAPTER 1

◆ Write the number.

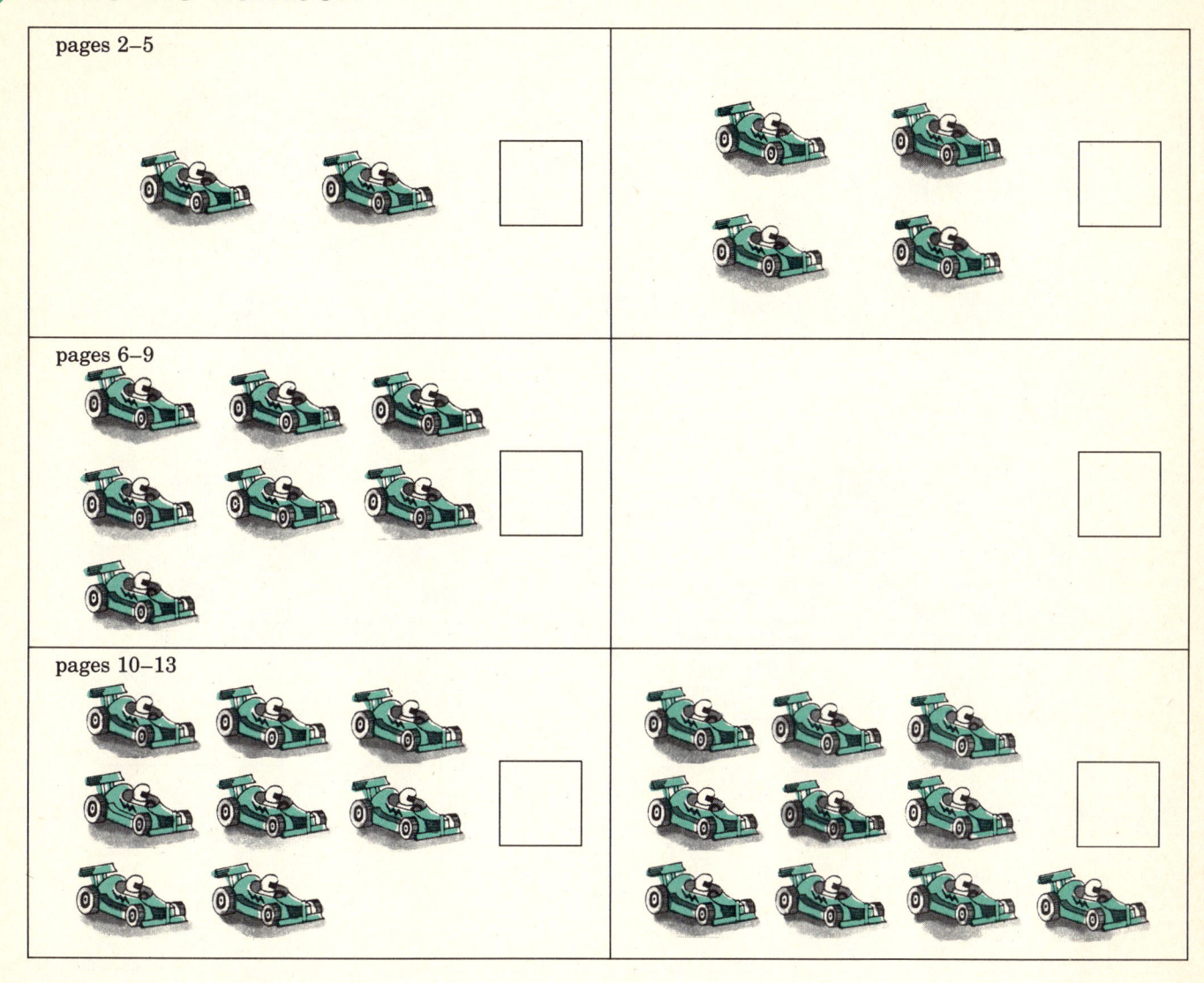

pages 2–5

pages 6–9

pages 10–13

◆ Write how much money. pages 14–15

147

Extra Practice

CHAPTER 1

◆ Count the pictures.
Write how many.

pages 16–17

148

Extra Practice

CHAPTER 2

◆ Add.

pages 24–27

2
+ 1
___

2
+ 2
___

5
+ 1
___

4
+ 3
___

pages 28–31

2
+ 0
___

0
+ 5
___

6
+ 2
___

5
+ 3
___

pages 32–35

7
+ 2
___

2
+ 8
___

6
+ 4
___

3
+ 6
___

◆ Write how much money.

pages 36–37

Extra Practice

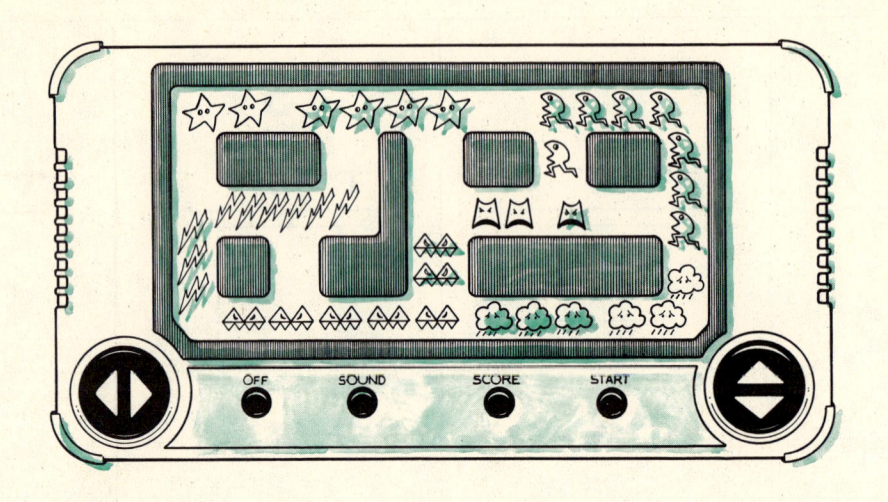

CHAPTER 2

◆Look at the picture.
Write how many. Add.

pages 38–39

Extra Practice

CHAPTER 3

◆ Subtract.

pages 46–49

| 4 − 1 = ☐ | 5 − 4 = ☐ | 7 − 3 = ☐ | 6 − 2 = ☐ |

pages 50–53

| 5 − 0 = ☐ | 1 − 0 = ☐ | 8 − 5 = ☐ | 8 − 2 = ☐ |

pages 54–57

| 9 − 6 = ☐ | 9 − 2 = ☐ | 10 − 5 = ☐ | 10 − 7 = ☐ |

◆ Write how much money.

pages 58–59

151

Extra Practice

CHAPTER 3

◆ Ring what comes next.

pages 60–61

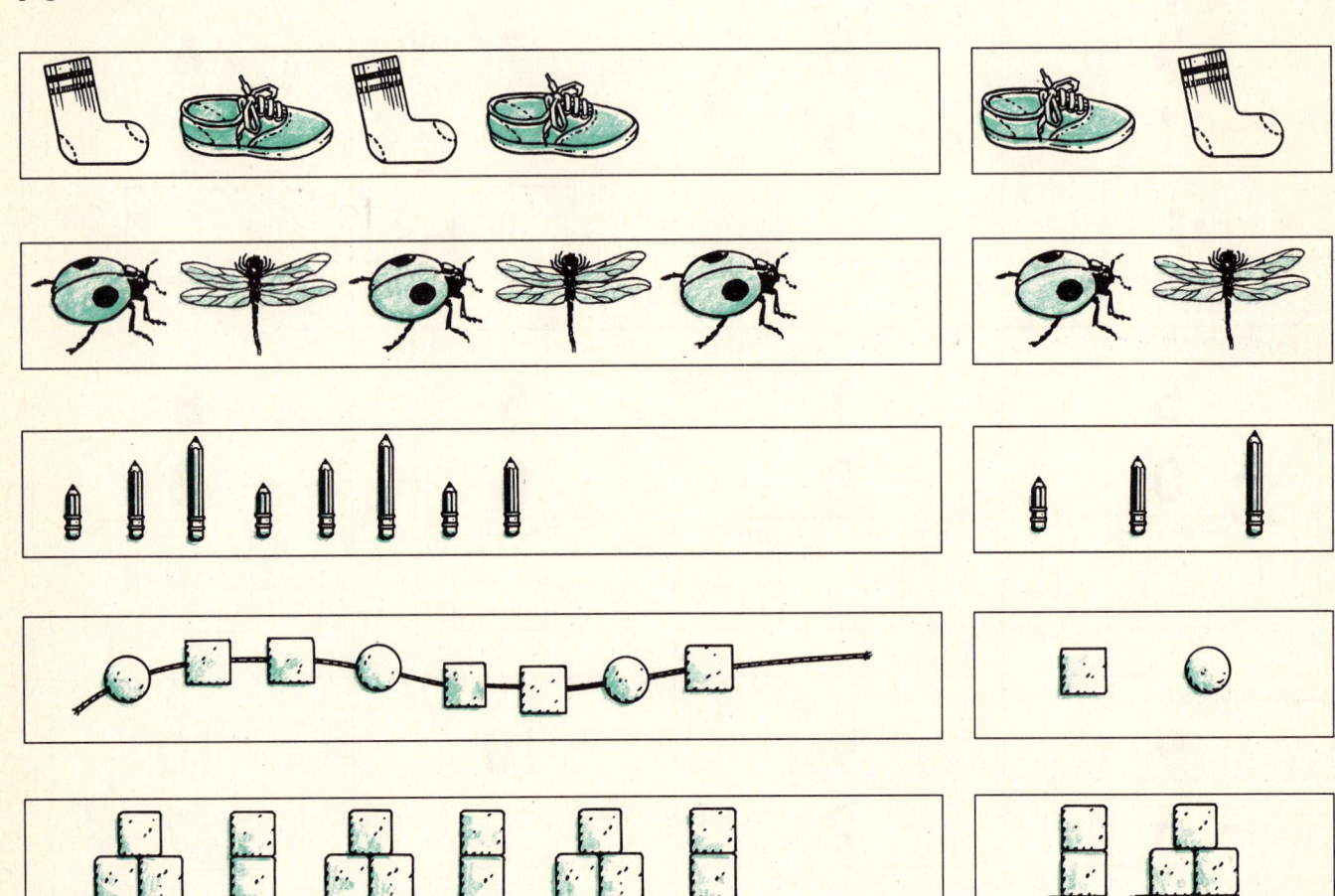

◆ Draw what comes next.

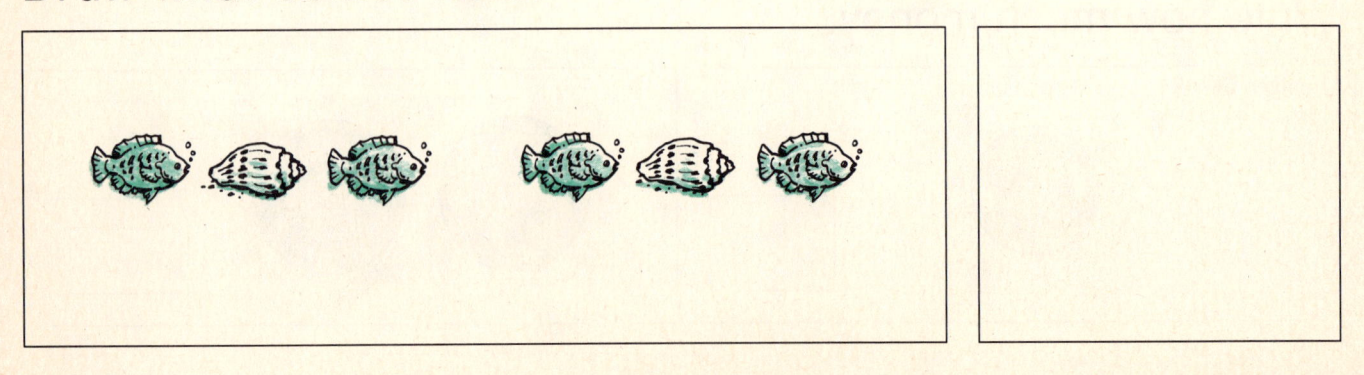

152

Extra Practice

CHAPTER 4

◆ How many?

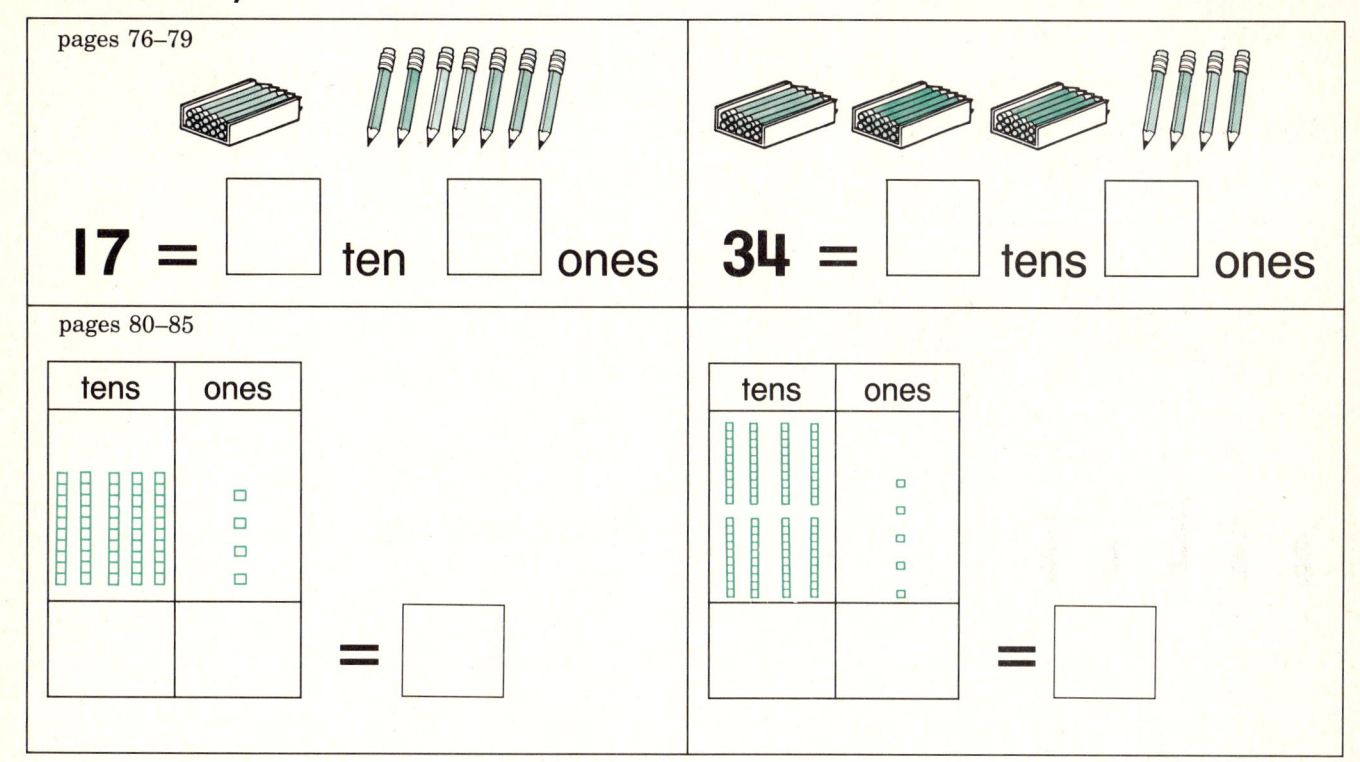

pages 76–79

17 = ☐ ten ☐ ones

34 = ☐ tens ☐ ones

pages 80–85

tens	ones

= ☐

tens	ones

= ☐

◆ Write each missing number.

pages 86–87

| 42 | | 44 | 45 |

| | 86 | | 88 |

◆ Write how much money.

pages 88–89

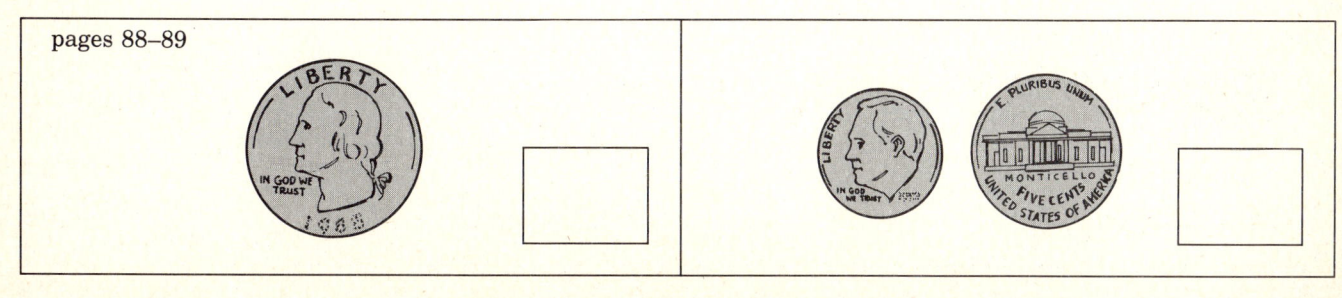

153

Extra Practice

CHAPTER 4

◆ Write the numbers to complete a pattern.
pages 90–91

| 56 | 58 | 60 | | | | 68 | | 72 | |

| 77 | 79 | | 83 | | | 89 | 91 | |

| 14 | 15 | 16 | | | 19 | | | |

| 55 | 60 | 65 | | | 85 | | | 100 |

| 10 | | | 40 | 50 | | | | 100 |

| 73 | 74 | 75 | 76 | | | | | |

◆ Use numbers to make a pattern of your own.

| | | | | | | | | | |

Extra Practice

CHAPTER 5

◆ **Add.**

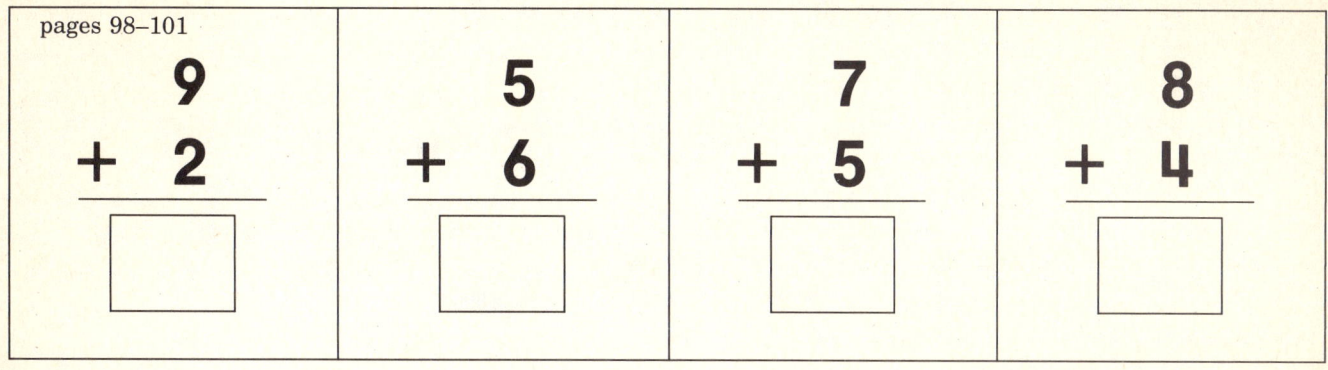

pages 98–101

```
  9        5        7        8
+ 2      + 6      + 5      + 4
```

◆ **Subtract.**

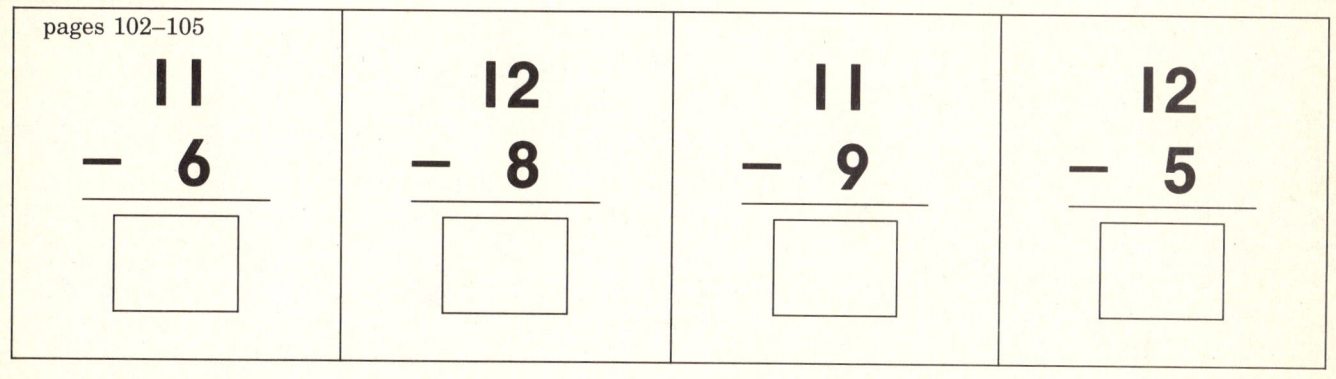

pages 102–105

```
 11       12       11       12
- 6      - 8      - 9      - 5
```

◆ **Mark the third** . pages 106–107

pages 108–109

Which is less?   6   9   Which is greater?   10   11

◆ **Write how much money.** pages 110–111

155

Extra Practice

CHAPTER 5

Ron made a graph to show the weather for one month.

Weather Graph

◆ Look at the graph.
Write how many of each.

pages 112–113

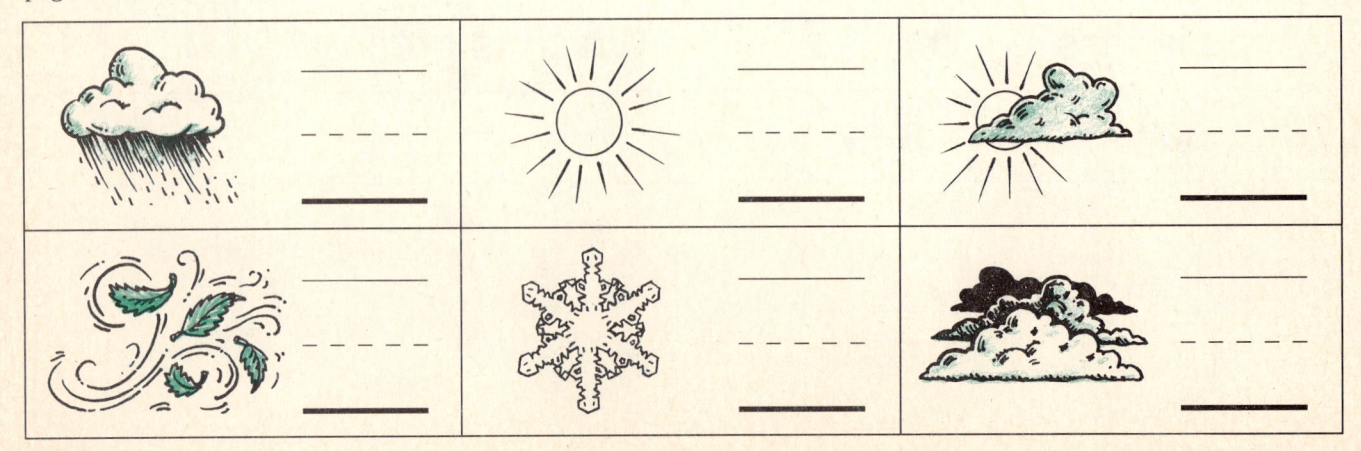

156

Extra Practice

CHAPTER 6

◆ Add.

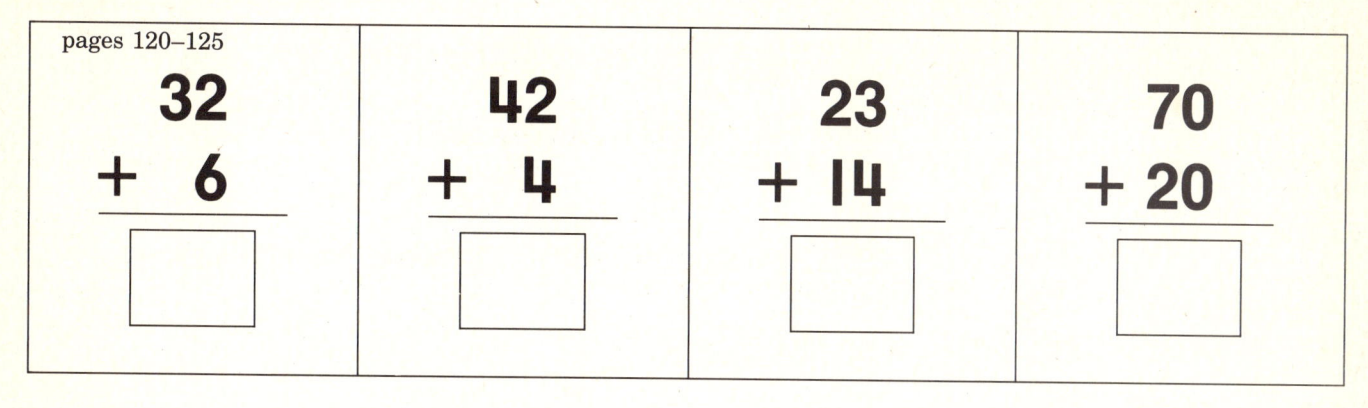

pages 120–125

32	42	23	70
+ 6	+ 4	+ 14	+ 20

◆ Subtract.

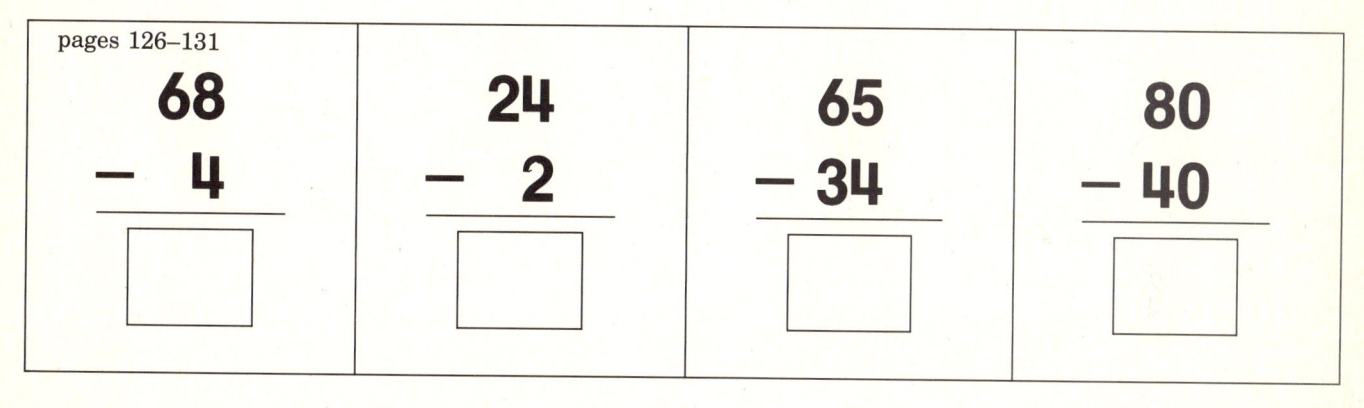

pages 126–131

68	24	65	80
− 4	− 2	− 34	− 40

◆ Write how much money.

pages 132–133

Extra Practice

CHAPTER 6

Mark asked his friends how they get to school. He made a graph to show their answers.

Getting to School

◆ Look at the graph. Write how many of each.

pages 134–135

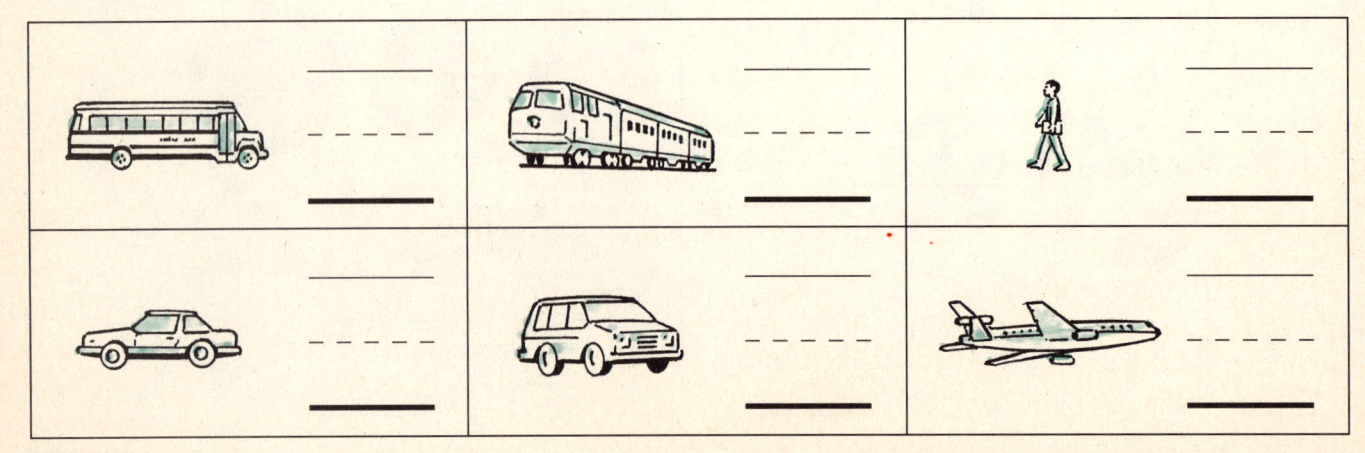